Quod scriptura, non iubet vetat

The Latin translates, "What is not commanded in scripture, is forbidden:'

On the Cover: Baptists rejoice to hold in common with other evangelicals the main principles of the orthodox Christian faith. However, there are points of difference and these differences are significant. In fact, because these differences arise out of God's revealed will, they are of vital importance. Hence, the barriers of separation between Baptists and others can hardly be considered a trifling matter. To suppose that Baptists are kept apart solely by their views on Baptism or the Lord's Supper is a regrettable misunderstanding. Baptists hold views which distinguish them from Catholics, Congregationalists, Episcopalians, Lutherans, Methodists, Pentecostals, and Presbyterians, and the differences are so great as not only to justify, but to demand, the separate denominational existence of Baptists. Some people think Baptists ought not teach and emphasize their differences but as E.J. Forrester stated in 1893, "Any denomination that has views which justify its separate existence, is bound to promulgate those views. If those views are of sufficient importance to justify a separate existence, they are important enough to create a duty for their promulgation ... the very same reasons which justify the separate existence of any denomination make it the duty of that denomination to teach the distinctive doctrines upon which its separate existence rests." If Baptists have a right to a separate denominational life, it is their duty to propagate their distinctive principles, without which their separate life cannot be justified or maintained.

Many among today's professing Baptists have an agenda to revise the Baptist distinctives and redefine what it means to be a Baptist. Others don't understand why it even matters. The books being reproduced in the *Baptist Distinctives Series* are republished in order that Baptists from the past may state, explain and defend the primary Baptist distinctives as they understood them. It is hoped that this Series will provide a more thorough historical perspective on what it means to be distinctively Baptist.

The Lord Jesus Christ asked, *"And why call ye me, Lord, Lord, and do not the things which I say?"* (Luke 6:46). The immediate context surrounding this question explains what it means to be a true disciple of Christ. Addressing the same issue, Christ's question is meant to show that a confession of discipleship to the Lord Jesus Christ is inconsistent and untrue if it is not accompanied with a corresponding submission to His authoritative commands. Christ's question teaches us that a true recognition of His authority as Lord inevitably includes a submission to the authority of His Word. Hence, with this question Christ has made it forever impossible to separate His authority as King from the authority of His Word. These two principles—the authority of Christ as King and the authority of His Word—are the two most fundamental Baptist distinctives. The first gives rise to the second and out of these two all the other Baptist distinctives emanate. As F.M. Iams wrote in 1894, "Loyalty to Christ as King, manifesting itself in a constant and unswerving obedience to His will as revealed in His written Word, is the real source of all the Baptist distinctives:' In the search for the *primary* Baptist distinctive many have settled on the Lordship of Christ as the most basic distinctive. Strangely, in doing this, some have attempted to separate Christ's Lordship from the authority of Scripture, as if you could embrace Christ's authority without submitting to what He commanded. However, while Christ's Lordship and Kingly authority can be isolated and considered essentially for discussion's sake, we see from Christ's own words in Luke 6:46 that His Lordship is really inseparable from His Word and, with regard to real Christian discipleship, there can be no practical submission to the one without a practical submission to the other.

In the symbol above the Kingly Crown and the Open Bible represent the inseparable truths of Christ's Kingly and Biblical authority. The Crown and Bible graphics are supplemented by three Bible verses (Ecclesiastes 8:4, Matthew 28:18-20, and Luke 6:46) that reiterate and reinforce the inextricable connection between the authority of Christ as King and the authority of His Word. The truths symbolized by these components are further emphasized by the Latin quotation - *quod scriptura, non iubet vetat*— i.e., "What is not commanded in scripture, is forbidden:' This Latin quote has been considered historically as a summary statement of the regulative principle of Scripture. Together these various symbolic components converge to exhibit the two most foundational Baptist Distinctives out of which all the other Baptist Distinctives arise. Consequently, we have chosen this composite symbol as a logo to represent the primary truths set forth in the *Baptist Distinctives Series*.

Baptism,
and the
Terms of Communion:
An Argument.

RICHARD FULLER, D.D.
1804-1876

BAPTISM,
AND THE
TERMS OF COMMUNION:
AN ARGUMENT.

BY
RICHARD FULLER.

With a Biographical Sketch of the Author by John Franklin Jones

THIRD EDITION

CHARLESTON, S.C.
SOUTHERN BAPTIST PUBLICATION SOCIETY,
229, KING-STREET
1854

he Baptist Standard Bearer, Inc.
NUMBER ONE IRON OAKS DRIVE • PARIS, ARKANSAS 72855

Thou hast given a *standard* to them that fear thee;
that it may be displayed because of the truth.
— *Psalm 60:4*

Reprinted 2006

by

THE BAPTIST STANDARD BEARER, INC.
No. 1 Iron Oaks Drive
Paris, Arkansas 72855
(479) 963-3831

THE WALDENSIAN EMBLEM
lux lucet in tenebris
"The Light Shineth in the Darkness"

ISBN# 1579784526

PREFACE.

In the following pages I have condensed several sermons preached, and now published, by request. Those who heard the discourses will bear me witness that I breathed not—for I am incapable of—an unkind thought towards my brethren who differ from me. Once, for all, let me say that I am a Baptist on principle, and not in sectarianism nor bigotry. I love all who love Jesus; but I do not love error, and cannot treat religious error, as if it were unimportant. The Pædobaptist works referred to in this treatise are full of harsh invectives against the Baptists; I hope that I have not emulated this temper. If, in any case, my language seem strong, it is directed solely against the error.

I need not remark how much indebted I am to those who have written on Baptism before me. I believe, however, that pastors will find this work meeting a want not hitherto met. The subject admits of demonstration. If I have failed in this demonstration, our Churches have many worthier sons who will "supply my lack of service." Should any one review this argument, I only ask that he will quote me fairly, and show me, as a brother, where the flaw is, and I will confess it.

I dedicate this essay to all, "of every name," who love truth more than party, and Christ more than a Church. The question is of vast importance to every man, especially to us ministers; since we are "set for the fall and rising of many," and cannot be in error without the fearful guilt of involving, or confirming, others, perhaps for generations to come, in error and disobedience.

CONTENTS.

PART FIRST.

THE ACT OF BAPTISM.

                                                                             Page.

The Commission—Baptizo is a Greek Word, with an English Termination.—It ought to have been Translated, - - 9

CHAPTER I.

The Word used for the Ordinance is Baptizo.—Dr. Porson's Opinion.—It has one Meaning.—Its Classical Use.—Concessions of Learned Pædobaptists, - - - - 12

CHAPTER II.

The Cases quoted by Pædobaptists to defend Sprinkling and Pouring.—The Plea that Words Change their Meaning; that Baptizo has a Sacred Meaning.—*Aggelos* and *Pneuma*.—Classical and Jewish Greek, - - - - 25

CHAPTER III.

Use of Baptizo in the Septuagint and Apocrypha.—Mr. Lape's Work on Baptism, - - - - - - 37

CHAPTER IV.

Figurative Use of Baptizo in the Greek Classics and the Septuagint.—A Question to Conscience.—Singular Pleas and Arguments.—Dr. Anthon's Letter, - - - . 46

CHAPTER V.

Use of Baptizo in the New Testament, when not applied to the Ordinance, - - - - - - - - 53

CHAPTER VI.

Use of Baptizo in the New Testament, when applied to the Ordinance.—Five Arguments, - - - - - 62

CHAPTER VII.

Allusions to Baptism in the New Testament.—Dr. Kurtz and Dr. Judson.—Pædobaptist Concessions, - - - 70

CHAPTER VIII.

Objections which have been attempted against Immersion.—Drs. Kurtz and Miller.—Baptism of the Three Thousand; of the Jailor.—Baptism in the Holy Spirit, - - - 77

CHAPTER IX.

The Greeks have always practised Immersion, and deride the idea of Sprinkling or Pouring, - - - - - 87

CHAPTER X.

History of Baptism, and the Substitution of Pouring and Sprinkling for Baptism.—Trine Immersion.—Clinics, - 91

CHAPTER XI.

Solemn Questions.—The Importance of the Subject, - 100

PART SECOND.

INFANT BAPTISN.

No Dispute as to Dedication, or Salvation of Infants.—Only Question is as to their Baptism, - - - - 107

CHAPTER I.

The Commission settles this Question forever.—The Pleas by

which this Demonstration has been met.—Those who introduced Infant Baptism confessed the necessity of Faith before Baptism.—Greek, Roman Catholic and Episcopal Churches.—Sponsors.—Infants received the Supper.—Luther and Calvin.—Modern Systems, - - - - 109

CHAPTER II.

Argument against Baptizing Infants from the Instances of Baptism in the New Testament.—The Plea from Household Baptism.—Dr. Kurtz's remarks on the Jailor's Household.—Dr. Miller's Assertion as to Households, - - 129

CHAPTER III.

The References to Baptism in the New Testament show that the Subjects were not Infants, - - - - - 143

CHAPTER IV.

If Baptism of Infants be a Duty, it is, of course, a Parental Duty, yet no such Precept among the Precepts to Parents.—Concessions, - - - - - - - 144

CHAPTER V.

Drs. Wood's and Stuart's concessions really surrender the whole question.—Passages from which inferences have been attempted in favor of Infant Baptism, - - 151

CHAPTER VI.

Arguments which have been fetched from the Old Testament.—Abrahamic covenant, - - - - - 162

CHAPTER VII.

Another Argument attempted from the Old Testament, viz: Sameness of the Jewish and Christian Churches.—The Pleas, that Christian Churches contain Unconverted Persons as well as the Jewish Nation.—That the Jewish Church had Greater Privileges than the Christian.—False Idea that Circumcision was itself a Privilege.—Another

Argument, viz: From Paul's language as to the Olive Tree, - - - - - . 175

CHAPTER VIII.
Argument formerly from pretended Jewish Proselyte Baptism.—This is Exploded, - - - - 183

CHAPTER IX.
Church History.—First Century; No Trace of Infant Baptism.—Second Century; No Trace of Infant Baptism.—Dr. Peters's Facts and Logic.—Mr. Slicer's Assertion as to Irenæus.—Proofs.—Concessions of Pædobaptists.—Tertullian.—Third Century; Infant Baptism creeps in with other Corruptions, but is plainly a perplexing innovation.—Fourth Century; Christianity thoroughly corrupt; yet, even at this time, Infant Baptism treated as an innovation.—This true even in the Fifth Century, - - - 185

CHAPTER X.
Easy to see how Infant Baptism would find its lodgment in Parental Feeling, as soon as impossibility of Salvation without Baptism was believed.—Manifold Evils of Infant Baptism.—Conclusion of Part Second, - - - 206

PART THIRD.

THE TERMS OF COMMUNION. OR THE RELATION OF BAPTISM TO THE SUPPER.

Baptists every where Spoken Against.—Charges Against Them.—Truth, Peace, Charity.—Charge of being a New Sect—Cardinal Hosius.—Mosheim.—Dr. Upeig.—Only Accusation with semblance of Reason is **Close** Communion, 215

Page.

CHAPTER I.

Word "Church" has two meanings in the Bible, viz: The Whole Body of the Regenerate, or a Particular Society.—A Third and Carnal Church, - - - - - 219

CHAPTER II.

Baptism an Individual Act.—The Supper a Social Ordinance belonging to the Visible Churches, and only for Members in those Churches.—Proofs, - - - - - 225

CHAPTER III.

Baptism a Prerequisite to Admission into a visible Church properly organized.—The Discussions about John's Baptism.—Proofs of the Proposition in this Chapter, - 229

CHAPTER IV.

Membership in some Pædobaptist Churches no Title to the Communion, for other reasons besides a want of Baptism, 236

CHAPTER V.

Various Arguments and Objections to Close Communion candidly considered. - - - - - - - 239

CHAPTER VI.

"*But we desire to hear of thee what thou thinkest; for as concerning this sect, we know that every where it is spoken against.*"—The Author begs leave to state frankly what he "thinks."—Christians should love each other, in spite of differences.—"Now we know in part"—"Soon we shall know, even as also we are known." - - - 246

PART FIRST.

THE ACT OF BAPTISM.

MARK xvi. 15, 16. "*And he said unto them, Go ye into all the world, and preach the gospel to every creature. He that believeth and is baptized, shall be saved; but he that believeth not* (it was unnecessary to add, *and is not baptized*, for he that believeth not will, of course, not be baptized, or if he be baptized, it will avail him nothing,) *shall be damned.*"

SAVED or damned! These are solemn thoughts, and solemnly should they be pondered by every man. The passage which you have just read is the Great Commission, the only authority by which ministers preach and baptize. If, therefore, one portion of the sacred oracles may be pronounced more important than any other, this is certainly the most important.

Now, it is deeply to be deplored that, in our English version of the Bible, one word of this Commission is not translated, but only transferred. This word is "Baptized." In the Greek original it is Baptistheis; so that, while all the other words of the Commission are rendered into English, this is not; we have only the Greek, with an English termination.*

The original word for "*Preach*" is *Kereuxate;* why

---

* Many Baptists insist that *baptize* is an English word, and means *immerse*. If this could be proved, it would shorten the argument. To me, it is plainly a transferred word. I cannot

did not the translators say, Go *Kereuxatize?* The Greek for "*Believeth,*" is *Pisteusas;* why did not the version read, He that *Pisteuseth?* This strikes us as absurd; yet no less absurd would it seem to an impartial person for "*Baptistheis*" not to be translated, but only transferred. I know that King James' version followed the Bishops' Bible, and the Bishops' Bible followed the Vulgate; but this does not mend the matter. A translation should be a transcript of the writer's meaning, as recorded in the original language, and when Jesus commanded men to be baptized, he employed a word in common use, perfectly well understood, and easily translated into any tongue.

Jesus says, "He that believeth, and is baptized, shall be saved." To charge him with wrapping up his meaning in an obscure phraseology, is impious; it is to accuse him of the enormous guilt of the Roman tyrant, who hung up his laws so high that people could not read them, and then inflicted punishment for their infraction. Besides, the Greek is the most perfect language ever spoken by man; but no written language, not even the Hebrew, is so imperfect that, when a lawgiver utters a command, his will cannot be clearly expressed. In short, *the translators of our Bible have,*

see that it ever had the *univocal* meaning of the Greek *baptizo.* In all translations of classical works, *Baptizo* is rendered Dip, Immerse. *Baptize* is only used in the Bible; and there the word *Baptizo* is translated in almost every instance where it *does not refer to the ordinance.* These facts prove that neither the translators of profane authors, nor the translators of our Bible, considered *baptize* as a translation.

themselves, exposed the pretext that there is any difficulty as to the word Baptizo. In the case of Naaman (2 Kings), the Septuagint uses Baptizo, and the translation renders it "dip." "Then went he down and dipped (Ebaptisato) himself seven times in Jordan."*

The non-translation of Baptizo imposes upon us the necessity of examining its meaning, and this I shall now do. That the question as to baptism excites so many bad passions is lamentable; it betrays an ulcerated state of feelings, which ought to fill us with concern and alarm. The matter before us is a calm philological inquiry as to the meaning of a Greek word; and I beg my reader to follow me with candor in the investigation.

---

* Dr. Campbell, Principal of the Marischal College, at Aberdeen, in Scotland, a minister of the Presbyterian Church, a scholar seldom equalled in extent and accuracy of theological investigation, expresses himself thus. (Prelim. Dissert. viii. Part ii. § 2.) "The word 'peritome,' the Latins translated circumcisio, (circumcision,) which exactly corresponds in etymology; but the word 'baptisma,' they have retained, changing only the letters from Greek to Roman. Yet the latter was just as susceptible of a literal version into Latin as the former. Immersio, (immersion,) answers as exactly in the one case as circumcisio, (circumcision,) in the other." "We have deserted the Greek names where the Latins have deserted them, and have adopted them where the Latins have adopted them. Hence we say circumcision, and not peritomy; and we do not say immersion, but baptism. Yet when the language furnishes us with materials for a version so exact and analogical, such a version conveys the sense more conspicuously than a foreign name. For this reason I should think the word immersion a better English name than baptism, were we now at liberty to make such a choice."

CHAPTER I.

The simple inquiry is, as to the meaning of the Greek word Baptizo; and in this chapter I shall examine its classical usage, that is, the sense in which the classical Greek authors employ it. In this examination let us not perplex a plain thing by any impertinent matter. The subject is too often involved in a cloud of criticisms about the import of the word Bapto. Now, we have nothing to do with Bapto. The Holy Spirit always, in speaking of the ordinance, uses one single word. That word is Baptizo, and to this let us confine ourselves.

That Bapto means to dip, and that Baptizo is a diminutive of Bapto, is an assertion sometimes very confidently made, but its authors only betray their innocence of the Greek language. In that language the addition of *zo* rather enforces, than diminishes, the primitive verb. It imparts a peculiar significancy, and seems generally to denote the transferring to another, or performing upon another, the thing designated. Thus *Oikeo*, to dwell; *Oikizo*, to make one dwell. *Sophos*, wise; *Sophizo*, to make wise. *Sophroneo*, to be of a sound mind; *Sophronizo*, to make one of a sound mind.

THE ACT OF BAPTISM. 13

And just so, *Bapto*, to dip; *Baptizo*, to make one dip, that is, to immerse. A similar termination seems to have a similar effect in the English language. As *Fertile; Fertilize. Grand; Aggrandize. Civil; Civilize.* Dr. Porson, the first Greek scholar England has ever produced, regarded Baptizo as more emphatical than Bapto.

"Not long before the death of Professor Porson," says Dr. Newman, "I went, in company with a much respected friend, to see that celebrated Greek scholar at the London Institution. I was curious to hear in what manner he read Greek. He, very condescendingly, at my request, took down a Greek Testament, and read perhaps twenty verses in one of the Gospels in which the word Bapto occurred. I said, 'Sir, you know there is a controversy among Christians respecting the meaning of that word.' He smiled and replied, 'The Baptists have the advantage of us.' He cited immediately the well known passage in Pindar, and one or two of those in the Gospels (mentioned in this letter). I inquired, whether, in his opinion, Baptizo must be considered equal to Bapto, which, he said, was to tinge, as dyers. He replied, to this effect, 'that, if there be a difference, he should take the former (Baptizo) to be the strongest.' He fully assured me that it signified a total immersion." This conversation took place August 27, 1807. See Carson, p. 23.

Where the ordinance is mentioned, Baptizo is always the word; and never was there a word the meaning of which was more clear and precise. Indeed if a word have not a precise meaning, how can language be the vehicle of our thoughts? The assertion, that Baptizo has three different meanings, only proves how strangely controversy can blind the mind to the plainest things. Suppose the word *saw*, meant *a saw*, and *an axe*, and *a nail;* how could a carpenter know what I mean, when I ask for a saw? To say, that a word means three distinct things, is to say that it means neither of them. If there were such a word, we would have to employ some other word to show which of the three things we intend. And this is true of the most general words. *Ride*, for example, means one thing; it means *ride*. You may ride in different ways; but it is still riding. *Ride* cannot mean *ride*, and *eat*, and *walk*.

The puerilities of which men are guilty on this plain matter are surprising. We are referred, for instance, in several treatises on baptism, to the word *spring*, as meaning *a leap*, and *a part of a watch*, and *one of the seasons*, and *a fountain of water*. A schoolboy, however, sees that these are different words, though similarly spelt, and, perhaps, traceable to the same origin. Words are the representatives of ideas. Suppose there were in Congress four brothers, representing different portions of the country; would he not be an idiot who should maintain that they were all the same man, because their names were spelt alike and they had a common parentage. If the Greek had been so imperfect that there were several verbs spelt *Baptizo*, yet having different significations, then one of these verbs might mean sprinkle. But this is not pretended.

THE ACT OF BAPTISM. 15

A similar folly has been again and again reiterated as to the words *wash* and *cleave*. It is said, that a command to *wash* is a command, either to *sprinkle*, or *pour*, or *dip*. I affirm that it is not a command to do either. It is a command to wash and nothing else. Washing is more than (and may be performed without) either *sprinkling* or *pouring* or *dipping*. Apply, now, these remarks to Baptizo. If it mean to *immerse*, then it does not mean *to sprinkle*, or *to pour*. You may be immersed in any manner you choose; but sprinkling and pouring are not modes of immersing.

The word *cleave*, which Dr. Beecher cites as having two meanings, proves what I affirm. Cleave, to *split*, is a *transitive* verb. Cleave, to *adhere to*, is *intransitive*. Confessedly two different words, though spelt alike.

The question before us, then, is this, What does Baptizo mean? I answer, it means *immerse*. It no more means to pour, or sprinkle, than it means to fly. This I affirm positively; and let no one charge me with presumption. Is it presumption to assert, that the English word *immerse*, means immerse and nothing else? But in Greek, Baptizo means immerse. Our opponents have been, over and over, defied to produce a single instance where it means sprinkle or pour. They have ransacked all the Greek writings, and have failed. They must forever fail. How fruitless would be a search in an English library, to find an instance where immerse means pour or sprinkle. And just such is the attempt to detect a passage in any Greek writer, by which our opponents can defend their practice as to baptism.

Out of hundreds of passages, I take, at random, the following, to show the import of Baptizo.

Orpheus, (Argn. 5 : 14,) "But when the sun had dipped himself (original, *baptized himself*) into the flood of the ocean, and the dark-shining moon lead in the stormy night, then went forth the warlike men who dwelt in the northern mountains."

Heraclides Ponticus, (Allegor. p. 495,)—"When a piece of iron is taken red hot from the fire, and is dipped (original, *baptized*) in water, the heat, being quenched by the peculiar nature of the water, ceases."

Pollybius L. 1, 51, describing a naval engagement between the Romans and Carthaginians, in which the latter were defeated, says that "on account of the weight of the vessels, and the unskilfulness of the rowers, they sunk (*baptized*) many of them." In L. 8. 8, relating the seige of Syracuse, he says : "The greater part of their vessels being sunk (*baptized*) they were filled with consternation." In L. 16. 16, speaking of the naval engagement between Philip and Attalus, which happened near Chios, he says : " Attalus seeing one of his quinqueremes (galleys with five oars in a seat) sunk (*baptized*) by one of the enemy's vessels," &c.

The Greek Scholiast on Euripedes, Hippol. 123,— "As when one dips (*baptizes*) the vessel iuto the fountain of water."

The Greek Scholiast on Aratus, 5. 951,—"The crow often dips (*baptizes*) herself from the head to the top of the shoulders in the river."

Alcibiades in Jacob's Anthol. 11. 49, note,—"And I,

plunging (*baptizing*) you in the waves of the sea, will destroy you in the briny surges."

Anacreon, in his Ode on Love in the heart,—"Finding Cupid among the flowers, I caught him and plunged (*baptized*) him into wine, and drank him up."

Æsop, in his fable of the Ape and the Dolphin, relates that the dolphin having generously undertaken to carry an ape ashore, who had been unfortunately wrecked at sea, became vexed with him for telling him a falsehood, and sinking (*baptizing*) him, " killed him :" that is, he plunged him under the water, till he was drowned. In his fable of the Shepherd and the Sea, he says: "The vessel being in danger of being sunk," (*baptized*,) &c.

Diodorus Siculus, L. 136, speaking of the sudden swelling of the Nile, says: "Many of the land animals are overtaken by the river, and being sunk (*baptized*) perish." In L. 11. 18, he says: "The Admiral's ship being sunk, (*baptized*,) the armament was thrown into great confusion." In L. 16. 80, he says: "The river rushing down with a violent current, sunk (*baptized*) many, and destroyed them."

From these examples it is manifest that Baptizo means to immerse, and no more means sprinkle, or pour, than the English word immerse does. If any one attempts to contradict this argument let him meet it fairly and honestly. Let him not, with Dr. Miller, deal in assertions without proof. Let him not say, " I can assure you that the word we render baptize does legitimately signify the application of water in any way as well as by immersion." Dr. Miller does not even attempt proof. Let no one thus mislead men in a matter of such moment as obedience to Jesus Christ. The question is one of fact. I demand proof to show that Baptizo ever means sprinkle or pour. If our opponents cannot bring this, they ought to surrender the question, and abandon the error. No one ought to substitute for proof his own assertion, or the assertions of others.

There is still another method of evading this question, which is even more reprehensible. It is the garbling an author's words, and thus misrepresenting him. Of this, Dr. Miller, with Mr. Burgess and others who servilely repeat Dr. Miller, has been guilty with reference to Mr. Carson. This writer affirmed that Baptizo means to immerse, and has no other meaning. On this point he says: "All the lexicographers are against him." But, now, how are they against him? Is it that they really assign to the word any such signification as sprinkling or pouring? Not at all. It is only that they multiply meanings unnecessarily, since all the meanings they give are really comprehended in one. Mr. Carson's own words are explicit, and ought to put to the blush those who have misrepresented him. "What an insurmountable task," says he, "would it be to master a language, if, in reality, words had as many different meanings as lexicons represent them! Parkhurst gives six meanings to Baptizo. I undertake to prove that it has but one; yet he and I do not differ about the primary meaning of this word. I blame him for giving different meanings, when there is no real difference in the meaning of this word. He assigns to it figurative meanings. I maintain, that in figures there is no different meaning of the word. It is only a figurative application. The meaning of the word is always the same. Nor does any one need to have a figurative application explained in any other way, than by giving the proper meaning of the word. When this is known, it must be a bad figure that does not contain its own light. It is useless to load lexicons with figurative applications, except as a concordance."*

Baptizo always denotes a total immersion. If only a part of a thing be immersed still it is an entire immersion of that part, and the context limits its extent. Thus, Polybius, 3. 72, "The foot soldiers passed through, (the water,) scarcely immersed (*baptized*) to the paps."

It has been said that baptize is a better word than immerse, because it signifies, not only an immersion, but an emersion, or rising again. This is a mistake. When Christ commands his disciples to be immersed, as a religious act, it is clear that they are not to be drowned. Baptizo, however, has nothing to do with the rising again. In many of the instances above given there was no rising again. The word, I repeat it, means nothing but immerse. No one word can express both an immersion and an emersion. Whether the thing immersed rises again, is to be gathered from the context. It will be time enough to show that the command of Christ requires an emersion, when I find a sect who drown the candidates. At present we have to do with our brethren

* Carson on Baptism, p. 57.

THE ACT OF BAPTISM.

who do not immerse. There will never be any difficulty about getting people out of the water; the only difficulty is to get them under it. The very nature of the object immersed may sometimes show that it does not remain sunk. Thus Plutarch, (in his Life of Theseus) when declaring that Athens may be plunged in calamity, but should not be ruined, quotes the Sybilline verse:—

"Thou mayest be immersed, (*baptized*,) O bladder, but it is not thy fate to sink."

The meaning is plain. A bladder filled with wind may be submerged, forced under the water; but it will rise again as soon as the force is withdrawn.

Having thus demonstrated what is the import of Baptizo, I shall now add the concessions of learned men in different ages. I shall not cite a single Baptist. Our opponents have a strange custom of quoting each other. When we accumulate the most overwhelming proof, and defy them to meet it, they reply by telling us what some writer of their own party has said. Dr. Kurtz cannot produce a single case, but tells us that "the editor of Calmet quotes some." Dr. Peters repeats Dr. Kurtz, and thus Doctors of Divinity echo and re-echo each other's unfounded assertions. I have established, beyond all controversy, what is the only meaning of Baptizo. If not a single opponent had ever conceded the point, that meaning would not be the less certain. It is, however, pleasing to find men overcoming their prejudices, and confessing the truth, though that truth condemns them. Out of many concessions, I give the following:

THE ACT OF BAPTISM.

Calvin.—"The word Baptizo signifies to immerse, and the rite of immersion was performed by the ancient Church."*

Luther.—"Baptism is a Greek word, and may be translated immersion, as when we immerse something in water, that it may be wholly covered. And although it is almost wholly abolished, (for they do not dip the whole children, but only pour a little water on them,) they ought, nevertheless, to be wholly immersed, and then immediately drawn out; for that the etymology of the word seems to demand."†

Beza, (on Mark vii. 4.)—"Christ commanded us to be baptized; by which word, it is certain, immersion is signified. Baptizesthai, in this place, is more than niptein; because that seems to respect the whole body, this only the hands. Nor does Baptizein signify to wash, except by consequence; for it properly signifies to immerse for the sake of dyeing. To be baptized in water, signifies no other than to be immersed in water, which is the external ceremony of baptism. Baptizo differs from the verb dunai, which signifies to plunge in the deep and to drown."‡

Vitringa.—"The act of baptizing is the immersion of believers in water. This expresses the force of the word. Thus also it was performed by Christ and his apostles."§

---
* Institutes, Lib. 4, chap. 15, § 19.
† Luth. Op., 1, p. 336.
‡ Epistola ii. ad Thom. Tilium. Annotat, in Marc. vii. 4, &c.
§ Aphor, Sanct. Theol. Aphoris. 884.

Hospinianus.—" Christ commanded us to be baptized, by which word it is certain immersion is signified."*

Gurtlerus.—"To baptize, among the Greeks, is undoubtedly to immerse, to dip; and baptism is immersion, dipping. Baptismos en Pneumatia agio, baptism in the Holy Spirit, is immersion into the pure waters of the Holy Spirit; for he on whom the Holy Spirit is poured out, is, as it were, immersed unto him. Baptismos en puri, 'baptism in fire,' is a figurative expression, and signifies casting into a flame, which, like water, flows far and wide; such as the flame that consumed Jerusalem. The thing commanded by our Lord is baptism; immersion into water."†

Buddeus.—"The words Baptizein and Baptismos, are not to be interpreted of aspersions, but always of immersion."‡

Salmasius.—"Baptism is immersion, and was administered in former times, according to the force and meaning of the word."§

Venema.—"The word Baptizein, to baptize, is no where used in the Scripture for sprinkling."‖

Professor Fritsche, a disciple of Hermann, (in his Com. on Matth. iii., 6.)—"Baptism was performed not by sprinkling, but by immersion; this is evident, not

* Hist. Sacram. L. ii. c. 1, p. 30.

† Institut. Theo. cap. 33, § 108, 109, 110, 115.

‡ Theolog. Dogmat. L. v. c. 1, § 5.

§ De Cæsarie Virorum, p. 669.

‖ Instit. Hist. Eccl. Vet. et Nov. Test. Tom. iii. sec. 1, § 138.

only from the nature of the word, but from Rom. vi. 4."

Augusti, vol. v. p. 5.—"The word Baptism, according to etymology and usage, signifies to immerse, submerge, &c.; and the choice of the expression betrays an age in which the latter custom of sprinkling had not been introduced."

Brenner, p. 1.—"The word corresponds in signification with the German word taufen, to sink into the deep."

The author of the Free Inquiry respecting Baptism, Leipsic, 1802.—"Baptism is perfectly identical with our word immersion or submersion (tauchen oder untertauchen.) If immersion under water is for the purpose of cleansing, or washing, then the word means cleansing or washing," p. 7. Again, "The baptism of John and that of the apostles were performed in precisely the same way; that is, the candidate was completely immersed under water." Speaking of Rom. vi. 4, and Gal. iii. 27, he says: "What becomes of all these beautiful images, when, as at the present day, baptism is administered by pouring or sprinkling?" p. 36.

Bretschneider.—"An entire immersion belongs to the nature of baptism." "This is the meaning of the word." "In the word Baptizo and Baptisma is contained the idea of a complete immersion under water; at least, so is Baptisma in the New Testament."*

This writer is confessedly the most critical lexicographer of the New Testament.

* Theology, Leipsic, 1830, vol. ii. p. 681.

Paullus, in his Com. vol. i. p. 278.—"The word baptize signifies, in Greek, sometimes to immerse, sometimes to submerge."

Rheinard's Ethics, vol. v. p. 79.—"In sprinkling, the symbolical meaning of the ordinance is wholly lost."

Scholz, on Matt. iii. 6.—"Baptism consists in the immersion of the whole body in water."

Professor Lange, on Infant Baptism, (1834,) p. 81.—"Baptism in the apostolic age was a proper baptism,—the immersion of the body in water." "As Christ died, so we die (to sin) with him in baptism. The body is, as it were, buried under water—is dead with Christ; the plunging under water represents death, and rising out of it the resurrection to a new life. A more striking symbol could not be chosen."

Bloomfield, in his Critical Digest on Rom. vi. 4.—"There is here plainly a reference to the ancient mode of baptism by immersion; and I agree with Koppe and Rosenmuller, that there is reason to regret it should have been abandoned in most Christian churches, especially as it has so evidently a reference to the mystic sense of baptism."

Neander, in his letter to Judd.—"As to your question on the original rite of baptism, there can be no doubt whatever that, in the primitive times, it was performed by immersion, to signify a complete immersion into the new principle of the divine life which was to be imparted by the Messiah."*

Edinburgh Ency.—"In the time of the apostles, the

---

* Judd's Reply to Stuart, p. 194.

form of baptism was very simple. The person to be baptized was dipped in a river or vessel, with the words which Christ had ordered, and, to express more fully his change of character, generally assumed a new name. The immersion of the whole body was omitted only in the case of the sick, who could not leave their beds. In this case sprinkling was substituted, which was called clinic baptism. The Greek church, as well as the schismatics in the East, retained the custom of immersing the whole body; but the Western church adopted, in the thirteenth century, the mode of baptism by sprinkling, which has been continued by the Protestants, Baptists only excepted."*

It was the complaint of a writer, that his opponent " did not know when a thing was proved." Every candid reader will, I think, grant that I have ascertained the meaning of Baptizo. It signifies to immerse, and has no other meaning. Indeed, if it means immerse, it cannot mean sprinkle or pour. These are entirely different actions.

CHAPTER II.

IF the meaning of Baptizo be so clear, how is it that so many learned and good men still persist in error? This is a question often put to us; it is, however, a question not for me, but for others. Any comparison between the error of my brethren on the subject of baptism, and the errors of Romanists, would be most unjust;

Edinburgh Ency. Art. Baptism.

it would wrong them, and wrong my own heart. Yet I may meet the above question by another. I ask, how was it, that learned and good men, like Thòmas a Kempis and Fenelon, could defend all the corruptions of the Church of Rome? Lord Bacon calls our prejudices "*the mind's idols;*" and who need be told that the most lodged and incurable prejudices are often found in men of erudition, whose piety we see and admire in many things.

Instead of dwelling on a matter which is painful and impertinent, let us take up at once the arguments of our opponents, and see what they are worth. As I before remarked, they have been challenged, over and over, to bring a single authority for their interpretation of Baptizo, and have signally failed. Nor has this been from any want of learning, or zeal, or research. It has been owing to the simple fact, that Baptizo means immerse and nothing else.

The first case urged by our opponents is from Dionysius of Halicarnassus (vit. Hom. p. 297). The critic is commenting on a passage in Homer (Ill. 16, 333), where Ajax stabs Cleobulus. Homer says: "He smote him in the neck with his hilted sword, and the whole sword became warm with blood." The meaning of this is plain. Ajax has his foe in his arms, and plunges his dagger, or short sword, into his neck, where it becomes warm in the blood. A few lines after, Homer, describing another conflict, says, of Peneleus: "He smote his (Lycon's) neck under the ear, and the whole sword plunged in." In commenting on the former of these passages, **Dionysius makes this remark**,—" Homer in this expression exhibits great energy, representing the sword as being so *baptized* as even to be warmed."

It is pretended that here *Baptizo* means smeared.— This is Professor Staurt's supposition. But it must be seen, by every reader, to be utterly unfounded. This interpretation destroys all the beauty of Homer's idea, which is not, that the dagger was warmed by blood remaining on it after it had been withdrawn from the neck, but that the dagger pierced the throat, and *there* being baptized (immersed) in the blood, became warm. Pope renders it,—

"Plunged in his throat, the smoking weapon lies."

This idea of warming a weapon in a wound is common among the ancient poets. Thus,—

Hor. Sermo 2, 3, 136.—" In matris jugulo ferrum tepefecit." " He warmed the steel in his mother's throat." Virg. Æn. 9. 418, 419,—"ut hæsta, trajectaque hæsit, tepefecta cerebro." " The spear flew, and sticking fast in the transpierced brain, became warm." Ibid. 5. 701. " Fixo ferrum in pulmone tepescit." " The steel became warm in his transfixed lungs." This case, then, cited by our opponents to show that Baptizo may mean something besides immerse, plainly recoils against them.

The next case, adduced also by Professor Stuart, is from Plutarch (Paralel. Græc. Rom. p. 545). Speaking of a Roman general who was dying of his wounds, Plutarch says: "He set up a trophy, on which, having *baptized* his hand in blood he wrote this inscription." Now

28   THE ACT OF BAPTISM.

here, again, how plain is it that this case makes against our opponents. Did the general sprinkle his hand in blood? or pour his hands in blood? Nothing can be more explicit. When we write, do we sprinkle or pour the pen in ink? We dip it; and just so here. The Roman dips his hand in blood, and writes. This case reminds me of a remark of that learned lawyer, Selden. " In England, of late years, I ever thought the parson baptized his own fingers, rather than the child."(Works, vol. 6, Col. 2008.)

The third case which our opponents have brought forward proves the indefatigable diligence with which they have explored every department of Greek literature for some authority. It is a medical prescription. Hippocrates (p. 254), speaking of a blister, says: "If it prove too painful, *baptize* it into breast milk and Egyptian ointment." His meaning is plain. It is that the violence of the blister shall be assuaged by dipping it in the milk and ointment. Hippocrates himself settles his meaning by the use of the same word in other places. Thus, p. 340, he compares a peculiar kind of breathing in some patients, to the manner of a person's fetching his breath after coming out from under the water. He says: " He breathed as persons do from being *baptized ;*" that is, from being immersed under the water. So, again, p. 357,—" He breathed just as persons do from *being baptized.*" Suppose we should read it, "He breathed as persons do from being wet, washed, or sprinkled;" where would be the propriety or the force of the expression? Immersion is the plain meaning. Again, p. 532,—" Shall I not laugh at the man who *baptizes* his ship by overload-

THE ACT OF BAPTISM.   29

ing it, and then complains of the sea for ingulphing it with its cargo?" Here, to baptize a ship is to sink it.

A fourth case cited by Pædobaptist authors is from Aristotle. It is produced to show that Baptizo does not always denote the act of plunging. My position is, that Baptizo means to immerse. It matters not how the immersion is effected. And the passage is conclusive against those who advance it. Here are the words of Aristotle (de Marabil Ause.) "Sailing beyond Hercules' Pillars, in four days, with the wind at east, they came to certain uninhabited places full of bulrushes and sea-weeds, which, when it is ebb-tide, are not overflowed, (*baptized*) but at full-tide are overflowed."

In searching the arguments of Pædobaptist writers to see what they can say, these are all the cases I have found; and my readers can now judge for themselves, whether these cases show that Baptizo means sprinkle or pour. There is one other case which has been urged. Our opponents tell us, that Origen says, of the wood and sacrifice of Elijah's altar, that "they were baptized." But as we are enquiring into the import of Baptizo at the time when the Saviour used it, and as Origen lived two hundred years after this period, I have not thought it worth while to examine this case. Suffice it to say that Origen's meaning is plain. The account is given in 1 Kings, xviii. and reads thus: "And Elijah took twelve stones, according to the number of the tribes of the sons of Jacob unto whom the word of the Lord came, saying, Israel shall be thy name. And with the stones he built an altar in the name of the Lord; and he made a trench about the altar, as great as would contain two measures of seed. And he put the wood in order, and cut the bullock in pieces, and laid him on the wood, and said, Fill four barrels with water, and pour it on the burnt sacrifice and on the wood. And he said, Do it the second time: and they did it the second time. And he said, Do it the third time: and they did it the third time. And *the water ran round about the altar; and he filled the trench also with water.*" Origen was one of the most impassionate of men; dealing in bold metaphors and allegories, and who but sees the force of his words? Did he mean that the altar was sprinkled? This will not be pretended. Did he mean that the altar was poured? This is absurd; for it was the water which was poured. What was the idea in Origen's mind? it was an immersion. The reason why the prophet ordered such an abundance of water to be poured, and why he filled the trench, was, to show the power of God; and who is surprised that a fervid writer or speaker should figuratively apply the term immerse to an altar surrounded with water, and bathed with water. We every day hear stronger language from men not at all very ardent.*

In this case we find an error into which Pædobaptist writers are constantly falling, and of which I will speak hereafter. If the word pour is used and the liquid is poured in such abundance that a baptism (immersion)

---

* Shakspeare makes Hamlet say,
"What would he do.
Had he the motive and the cue for passion
That I have? He would *drown* the stage with tears.'

follows, they cry out, There! how plain it is, that to pour, and to baptize, are the same thing. To which I answer, how plain it is that they are not the same thing; for the pouring takes place first, and the baptism afterwards. Whenever we use a baptistery the water is first poured into the font; but is this the baptism? The baptism follows when the candidates are immersed. Suppose a man should lie in the baptistery while it is filling. The pouring of the water would not be immersion, yet an immersion would take place if he remained long enough. In the case of Elijah, the twelve barrels of water were first poured, and the trenches all around filled, and it is the effect of this, it is the thus being drenched, surrounded, and steeped, which Origen figuratively calls a baptism.

In commanding his disciples to be baptized, Jesus knew what act he enjoined, and he could have been at no loss for a word clearly to express his meaning. Did he intend *Sprinkling?* the word was *Rantizo.* Did he require *Pouring?* the word was *Keo.* If *Wash; Nipto.* If *Bathe; Louo.* If *Immerse or Dye,* (the word having this latter meaning because dyeing is by immersing,) *Bapto.* If Jesus meant *immerse, and nothing else,* the word was *Baptizo.* This is the word he has used, and which the Holy Spirit always employs, when the rite of baptism is mentioned.

To maintain their position, our opponents sometimes resort to arguments which are most singular. For example, it is said that words change their meaning in the process of time. Admitted. I can furnish these writers with a stronger instance than any they have mentioned.

The word *let* formerly signified *hinder*,* now it means *permit*. But where is the evidence that the signification of Baptizo ever changed? Not a particle of proof is adduced. As I mean, however to meet even the cavils by which the popular mind has long been misled on the subject, I will presently settle this point. The authorities hitherto cited by me have been from classical writers before the apostolical age. I will directly cite Greek authors who were of that age and the ages succeeding; and thus I will prove the negative, and show that the word meant immerse, not only before, but during, and after the days of Christ and the Apostles.

Another plea, sometimes urged, would be amusing, if the subject were not too solemn. It is, that Baptizo has a *sacred meaning*; that is to say, it meant immerse until Jesus used it, and then, all at once, it got to mean something else. If this absurdity were admitted, it would make the Scriptures utterly worthless, since nobody could know what Jesus meant. When he said, "Blessed are the meek," "Blessed are the merciful," the words "meek," and "merciful," may have acquired a new meaning as soon as he uttered them, and perhaps may mean "proud" and "vindictive." And just so with all his sayings. His words would not only furnish no clue to his meaning, but serve really to deceive us. I was wrong, just now, to speak of his sophistry as ridiculous; it is an impiety which ought to fill a pious mind with horror.

* "Unhand me, gentlemen,
I'll make a ghost of him that *lets* me."—HAMLET.

THE ACT OF BAPTISM.

These remarks apply to two words which are said to have acquired new meanings as soon as Jesus used them, viz: *Aggelos*, angel, and *Pneuma*, spirit. It is affirmed that the former meant "messenger," and the latter "wind." I answer, *Aggelos* is simply a term of office, the context deciding its import in each case. It is frequently applied, in the New Testament, to a common messenger. As Luke ix. 52,—"He sent messengers (*aggelous*) before his face," &c. *Pneuma* meant spirit when Christ used it. Æschylus and other classical Greek writers employ it in this sense. See Donnegan's Lexicon.

The only other plea of our opponents is, some difference between classical Greek and the Greek spoken by Jews. But this is, if possible, even flimsier than the other pretexts just mentioned. As usual, it is a bold assertion without even an attempt at proof, and we have abundant evidence that the Jewish writers used the word *Baptizo* in the same sense with the Greeks. The subjoined quotations, from the Septuagint, and from Josephus, the most celebrated Jewish writer of that day, settle this matter. I add, too, other quotations bearing on each of the three fallacies I have been exposing.

The Septuagint is a Greek translation of the Old Testament. It was made about two hundred and seventy years before Christ, and by Jews, and is quoted by the Saviour and the Apostles. Now in this version the Hebrew word, meaning *Dip*, is translated by *Baptizo*. I allude to the case of Naaman already cited.

Josephus, contemporary with the Apostles, says (in his own Life,) "Our vessel being sunk (*baptized*) in the midst of the Adriatic, we swam all night, until the break of day, when we discovered a vessel of Cyrene, and myself, with certain others, to the number of eighty, were taken on board." In Ant. 9–10. 2, giving an account of the storm that overtook Jonah, he says: "The storm increasing the vessel just going to be sunk, (*baptized*) and being entreated by the Prophet, as well as fearing for their own safety, they cast him into the sea." In Ant. 15. 3, 3, speaking of the death of Aristobulas, one of Herod's sons, he says: "They decoyed him into a pool, and, as he was swimming, kept pressing him down and submerging (*baptizing*) him until they quite drowned him." Josephus mentions the same transaction in his Bell. Jud., Book i. 22, 2, where he says: "The lad was sent to Jericho by night, and there perished, being sunk (*baptized*) in a pool by the Gauls, according to Herod's command." Again, Josephus, Bell. ii. 18, 4, relating the account of one Simon, says, that after killing his father and mother, wife and children, to prevent their falling into the hands of the enemy, "he plunged (*baptized*) the whole sword into his own throat."

In Bell. ii. 20, 1, he says: "After Cestius was overthrown, many of the most eminent of the Jews swam away from the city, as from a ship that is being sunk" (*baptized*.) In Bell. iii. 7, 5, he says: "I should esteem that pilot to be an arrant coward, who, out of fear of a storm, should sink (*baptize*) his vessel of his own accord." In Bell. iii. 10, 9, describing an engagement between the Jews and Romans, he says: "If the Jews ventured to come near the Romans, they were sunk (*baptized*) together with the ships themselves." Again, directly after, describing some who were perishing in the water, he says: "If any of those that were submerged (*baptized*) raised their heads above the water, they were either killed by darts, or caught by the vessels."

Strabo, contemporary with Christ, L. vi. speaking of a lake near Agrigentum, in Sicily, says: "Things that usually do not swim, are not sunk (*baptized*) in the waters of this lake, but float like wood." Baptism is here opposed to floating; that is, it means immersion or sinking. In L. xii. speaking of a certain river in Cappadocia, he says: "If one shoots an arrow into it, the force of the water resists it so much that it will hardly be sunk," (*baptized*.) Again, in the same book, speaking of a marsh or lake called Tatta, he says: "The water readily coagulates about every thing that is immersed (*baptized*) into it." In L. xiv. he says of Alexander's soldiers: "they marched a whole day through the water, immersed, (*baptized*) up to the waist." In L. xvi. he says of the lake Sirbo: "The bitumen floats upon the surface, because of the nature of the water, which does not admit of diving: nor can any one who goes into it be immersed, (*baptised*) but is borne up."

Epictetus (about A. D. 68,) vol. 3, p. 69, says: "As you would not wish to sail in a large and finely ornamented vessel and be sunk (*baptized*,) so neither would you choose to live in a large and richly furnished house and be in a storm."

Plutarch (A. D. 50,) in his Treatise de Superstitione, says: "Plunge (*baptize*) yourself into the sea, and sitting down on the ground remain all day." In vol. 10,

p. 108, he speaks of a person "plunging (*baptizing*) himself into the lake Copais." In his life of Sulla, (21,) speaking of the battle of Orchomenus, he says that many weapons of the barbarians, such as bows, helmets and swords, were to be found in his time "buried (*baptized*) in the marshes." In his life of Alexander, (67,) speaking of his bacchanalian procession in Carmania, says: "In the whole company there was not to be seen a buckler, a helmet or spear; but all the way the soldiers dipping (*baptizing*) with cups, flagons and goblets out of large casks and urns, drank to each other; some as they were marching along, and others as they were seated at tables." Dipping wine out of casks and urns is here called baptizing out of casks and urns.

Pliny, (A. D. 100,) L. 11. Epis. 17, describing his country seat, says: "*Inde balieni cella frigidaria spatiosa et effusa, cujus in contrariis parietibus duo* BAPTISTERIA *velut ejecta sinuantur abunde capacia, si* INNARE *in proximo cogites.*"—Of which, Melmouth, the translator of Pliny, gives the following version. "From thence you enter into the grand and spacious cooling room belonging to the baths, from the opposite walls of which two round BASONS project, large enough to SWIM in."

Lucian, (A. D. 135,) in his Dialogue of Timon the man-hater, makes him say: "If the winter torrent should carry any one away, and he should with outstretched hands beg to be taken out, I would press upon his head, submerging (*baptizing*) him until he would rise no more." Again, in the second book of his "True Narrative," this writer mentions the discovery of a sea of milk, and an island of cheese. and next a multitude of men running upon the water, who were in all respects like other people, except their feet, which were of cork. He says: "We were astonished to see that they were not sunk (*baptized*,) but ran over the waves without fear."

Dio Cassius, (A. D. 155,) L. 5, 18, asks: "How could the vessel escape being sunk (*baptized*) by the very multitude of rowers?" In L. 37, 15, he says: "So great a storm arose suddenly through the whole country that the vessels in the Tiber were sunk (*baptized*.)" In L. 41, 42, relating the defeat of Curio by Juba, he says: "Many of them perished in their flight, being pushed into the sea by the crowd as they were entering the ship, and some being sunk (*baptized*) with the ships themselves, on account of their being overladen."

Porphyry, (A. D. 233,) Peristugos, p. 282, in his story of the trial of accused persons in the invisible world, by making them pass through the river Styx, says: "When the accused person enters it, if he is innocent, he passes safely, having the water up to his knees; but if he is guilty he proceeds but a little way before he is sunk (*baptized*) up to his head."

CHAPTER III.

OUR disquisition thus far into the import of the word *Baptizo* ought to put an end to this controversy. In this chapter I wish to examine its use in the Septuagint and the Apocrypha.

The Septuagint, as I have already remarked, is a Greek

version of the Old Testament. Of its value we may judge from the fact, that it is often cited in the New Testament.

In the Septuagint, *Baptizo* occurs only twice, once literally and once figuratively. The figurative use of the word I shall hereafter consider. The instance where it occurs literally is in the history of Naaman before mentioned, and I ask, does not this establish the meaning of the word? Here, in a work known by Jesus, and cited by him, we find *Baptizo*, and it is admitted, on all hands, to mean *immerse*. Jesus uses the same word, and thus commands the very same act. Can a candid man longer doubt what he means? "Naaman went down and dipped himself (Ebaptizato) seven times in the Jordan." All concede that this was immersion. Now Jesus commands this very act. Indeed, it was in this very river that John baptized, and the very phraseology is used in the accounts of some of the baptisms in the New Testament. The Septuagint says, Naaman " *Ebaptizato en to Jordane.*" This is admitted to mean, Naaman " dipped himself in the Jordan." In Matt. iii. 6, we are told that the people " *Ebaptizonto en to Jordane,*" the very same expression. Yet it is affirmed this means they stood on the bank and were sprinkled! Again, the Septuagint says, Naaman " *Katebe kai Ebaptisato ;* and this is admitted to mean, Naaman " went down and dipped." But in Acts viii. 38, it is said of the Eunuch and Philip that they both " *Katebesan eis to udor,*" (the very verb,) it is pretended that *Katebesan* only means, went to the edge of the water!

The Apocryphal books are certain works existing in

THE ACT OF BAPTISM. 39

the time of Christ. The Church of Rome affirms that some at least of these productions are inspired, but this has been over and over disproved. They are, however, very ancient, and are often bound in the same volume which contains the Old and New Testaments.

These writings were by Hebrew authors, and are in the Greek language. Does *Baptizo* occur here? It does in two passages, which I will now examine.

The first passage is in Judith xii. 7, 8, "Then Holofernes commanded his guard that they should not stay her. Thus she abode in the camp three days, and went out in the night into the valley of Bethulia and washed (*baptized*) herself in a fountain of water by the camp. And when she came out, she besought the Lord," &c. Here the expression is the very same as that used with reference to Naaman's dipping himself; and is not the passage equally plain? Observe, Holofernes had ordered the soldiers to let her pass whenever she choose. She was very devout, and frequently performed religious ceremonies. All this appears from the whole history. At this time a peculiar strictness is required, for she is purifying herself for a great and glorious deed. She, therefore, selects the night, and attended, probably, by her waiting woman, who had come to the camp with her, she bathes in a fountain situated in the valley of Bethulia. The pretence that bathing would have been indelicate is absurd. Had it been in the day, and in a place where our heroine could be seen, there would have been no indelicacy, for she was, of course, dressed in proper apparel.

Maimonides, as quoted by Lightfoot, on Matt. iii. 6,

observes, "If any one should enter into the water with their clothes on, yet their washing holds good, because the water would pass through their clothes, and their garments would not hinder it."

But when we remember that it was night, and in a sequestered valley, this squeamishness is simply foolish. As if to leave no doubt, however, as to her bathing, it is expressly said that "she came out of the water." Indeed, this very case is cited by Spencer, in his learned work on the Hebrew rites, to prove that the Jews, as well as the Gentiles, bathed their whole persons when about to perform religious vows. He says "that the Jews also" (that is, as well as the Gentiles) " when about to perform their vows sometimes cleansed their whole body in a bath, I gather from the history of Judith, who, when she had resolved to pray, is said to have baptized herself in a fountain of water." De Leg. Heb. Rit. p. 789. Judœos etiam, vota facturos, quandoque totum corpus lavacro purgasse, ex historia Judithæ colligo, quæ, cum precari statuisset, aquæ fonte seipsam baptizasse dicitur.

The other case is in Ecclesiasticus, xxxiv. 25. In our version it reads thus: "He that washeth himself (*Baptizomenos*) after touching a dead body, if he touch it again what availeth his washing?" Such are the words, and our opponents have attempted to lay this passage under contribution. To give a specimen of the sort of reasoning found in too many of their essays, I will quote from a volume printed in this city. The work before me is called "Christian Baptism." It is by the Rev. Thomas Lape, A. M., and is recommended in the highest terms by one Synod, and I know not how many Doctors of Divinity. It is printed both in German and English, has passed through four editions, and is, therefore, no common production. Of the author I know nothing, and allude not to him, but to his book, which is too bad. I may expose other portions of this essay hereafter, at present I give the author's argument on the passage we are examining.

"In the *classic Greek* of the Old Testament," says Mr. Lape, "we have several striking instances. In Ecclesiasticus, xxxiv. 25, the son of Sirach, speaking of one who had been purified from the pollution of a dead body, says: 'He was baptized from the pollution of the dead.' The question arises, how was an individual purified from the pollution of the dead? In the book of Numbers, xix. 13, we read as follows: 'Whosoever toucheth the dead body of any man that is dead, and purifieth not himself, defileth the Tabernacle of the Lord; and that soul shall be cut off from Israel; because the water of separation was not sprinkled (*baptized*) upon him, he shall be unclean; his uncleanliness is yet upon him.' Here you perceive this baptism was expressly performed by sprinkling water upon him. Evidently here Baptizo cannot mean to immerse, but to sprinkle."

Now I say nothing of this writer's placing Ecclesiasticus, an Apocryphal book, in the sacred canon, nor of his talking about the "classic Greek of the Old Testament," when every body knows that the Old Testament was written in Hebrew. This is little compared with two assertions which are amazing. First, this writer, in quoting Numbers, xix., declares that the word "*sprinkled*" is, in the original, "*baptized*." The word in the Septuagint is *Perierrantisthe;* from *rantizo*, to *sprinkle.* What will my readers say to this?

This is not the worst. The question, as Mr. Lape says, is as to the purification of one who had touched a dead body; and, now, this very 19th chapter of Numbers settles the whole question by requiring the person, after being sprinkled, to bathe, before he could be clean. The law of the case before us is as follows:

Numbers, xix. from v. 16 to 20,—"And whosoever toucheth one that is slain with a sword in the open fields, or a dead body, or a bone of a man, or a grave, shall be unclean seven days. And for an unclean person they shall take of the ashes of the burnt heifer of purification for sin, and running water shall be put thereto in a vessel: And a clean person shall take hyssop and dip it in the water, and sprinkle it upon the tent, and upon all the vessels, and upon the persons that were there, and upon him that touched a bone, or one slain, or one dead, or a grave: And the clean person shall sprinkle upon the unclean on the third day, and on the seventh day: and on the seventh day he shall purify himself, and wash his clothes, *and bathe himself in water*, and shall be clean at even."

Immersion was required even when any vessel touched a dead body, as is plain from Levit. xi. 32.—"And upon whatsoever any of them, when they are dead, doth fall, it shall be unclean; whether it be any vessel of wood, or raiment, or skin, or sack, whatsoever vessel it be, wherein

THE ACT OF BAPTISM. 43

any work is done, it must *be put into water*, and it shall be unclean until the even; so it shall be cleansed."

Indeed, Maimonides (Lightfoot on Matt. iii. 6,) says: "Wheresoever in the law, washing of the body or garments is mentioned, it means nothing else than the washing of the whole body. For if any wash himself all over except the very top of his little finger, he is still in his uncleanness." Lightfoot on Mark, vii. 4, produces also, from another Jewish writer, a sentence which shows that pollution occasioned by the touch of the dead, was so great that the person "must plunge his whole body."

The case of Naaman is exactly in point. Naaman was a leper. He is commanded to "*wash*." He goes down and *dips*. Even if we had not the above conclusive explanation of the meaning of the word "*wash*" in Ecclesiasticus, who, after this, could doubt whether the washing was an immersion, or a sprinkling, or pouring?

As this work of Mr. Lape' has been so industriously extolled and read, I must be pardoned for quoting two other examples which the author adduces from "the classical Greek of the Old Testament," and which, he says, "fully illustrate and confirm his position that it (Baptizo) has other meanings than immersion." I give his own words, begging those who may review me to do likewise.

"In Leviticus, xiv. 6, we have the following language: 'As for the living bird, he (the priest) shall take it, and the cedar wood, and the scarlet, and the hyssop, and shall dip (*baptize*) them and the living bird in the blood of the bird that was killed over the running water.' Now I appeal to the conscience of any man, is it possible that the cedar wood, the scarlet, the hyssop, and the living bird, could all be immersed in the blood of a single bird? There would only be blood enough to stain them, or in common language, to render them bloody. Here, then, the word Baptizo cannot mean to immerse, but only to stain or color.

"In the book of Dan. iv. 33, we have a description of the insane king of Babylon given, that he was baptized with the dew of heaven, in the following language: 'And his body was wet (*baptized*) with the dew of heaven.' Here there can be no immersion. Immersion signifies the sinking of a body in water, but here you perceive that the dew of heaven fell upon him. The word Baptizo here evidently then cannot mean to immerse, but to bedew or sprinkle. Many more instances from the Greek of the Old Testament might to be quoted to confirm my position, but I pass on to the New Testament."

Mr. Lape affirms that the original word in both these passages is *Baptizo*—an assertion which is doubly untrue. For, first, the original is Hebrew, whereas Baptizo is Greek! And, secondly, even in the Greek Septuagint, the original is not *Baptizo* but *Bapto*, a word which means to *Dye*.

If the Septuagint had employed *Baptizo* in the case from Daniel, it would only have been an intensive metaphor like this in Milton—

> "A cold shuddering dew
> *Dips* me all o'er."

But the term used is not *Baptizo*—it is *Bapto*.

This is not all. In the first case not only has the writer made a misstatement as to the verb, but he misrepresents the Scriptures. If my readers will refer to the chapter, they will see that water was to be taken from a running stream in some vessel, and into this water the blood of the bird was to fall. Into this vessel the dipping was to be performed. In verses 50 and 51, this is explained. There the blood and water (designed as emblems of Christ's atonement, which secures pardon and purity) are found to be enough, not only for the dipping of the cedar wood, &c. into it, but for sprinkling the house seven times. Nothing can be more explicit than this chapter. First, the blood is poured into a vessel of running water. Then, the things are dipped. Lastly, the defiled objects are sprinkled. That Mr. Lape designed any perversion of God's word, I do not affirm. I assail nobody's sincerity; but his entire ignorance of the import of the chapter is inexcusable.

The assertion, as to "many more instances," ought not to have been made. There is not a shadow of truth in it, and how awful a thing thus to misguide men as to a solemn ordinance of the gospel. When we come to the New Testament I shall again notice this work, with others. At present I leave it, and here end this chapter, in which I have proved that in the Septuagint and Apocrypha, composed by Jews, in the language of the New Testament, and existing in the time of Christ—the word *Baptizo* has but one meaning, and always signifies *immerse*.

CHAPTER IV.

In this chapter I will speak of the figurative use of *Baptizo* by Greek authors, and in the Septuagint and Apocrypha. When a word is employed figuratively, not only is no new signification attached to it, but the whole force of the metaphor depends on our knowing and recollecting the literal meaning.

In English we say, *Plunged in grief; Immersed in business; Buried in sleep.* In these cases the verbs are used figuratively, but we can only comprehend the figure, by knowing the literal import of the verbs. Our poets sometimes allow themselves great license, but the original idea is still retained. Thus Milton, as already cited:—

"A cold shuddering dew
Dips me all o'er."

Could such an instance of the use of *Baptizo* be found in any Greek poet, how would the advocates of sprinkling exult! Yet what would we think of one who should affirm that, in English, "*Dip*," means sprinkle? Again, Cowley (Dav. Book ii.) has these lines:—

"Still doth he glance the fortune of that day
When *drowned* in his own blood Goliath lay."

And Shakspeare thus writes:—

"What would he do,
Had he the motive and the cue for passion
That I have? He would drown the stage with tears."

Every body understands these sentences, and yet had *Baptizo* been used as *drown* is here, our opponents would pronounce the evidence conclusive. "It is clear," they would exclaim, "that the word means *wash* and *sprinkle*, for how can a man be immersed in his own blood, or a stage be immersed in tears?"

Having made these observations, let us now come to the verb *Baptizo*, and it is remarkable that all the research of our Pædobaptist brethren has failed to find even a metaphorical license by which to give a semblance of plausibility to their error. Here are specimens of the figurative use of the word among classic, Jewish, and patristic authors. If my readers will substitute *sprinkle*, or *pour*, for baptize, they will see the glaring fallacy I am combating.

Evenus, in Anthol, ii. 49, says: "Bacchus (or wine) immerses (*baptizes*) one in a sleep like that of death;" i. e. "drunkenness sinks one into a death-like sleep."

Josephus, Art. x. 9, 4, says, "that Ishmael, who was sent by the king of the Ammonites to kill Gedaliah, seized his opportunity when he saw him "by drunkenness sunk (*baptized*) into insensibility and sleep."

Clemens Alexandrinus, Pœd. ii. 2.—"He is a sluggard, who instead of watching unto wisdom, is by drunkenness, sunk (*baptized*) into sleep."

Heliodorus, Æthiop. L. iv. 17.—"When midnight had sunk (*baptized*) the city in sleep." This is the very figure of Virgil (Æn. ii. 265) where, speaking of the capture of Troy, by the Greeks, he represents the City as "*Buried in sleep and wine.*"

Plutarch, Conviv. L. 3, 9, 8, 7, says of those who are slightly intoxicated: "Their mind only is disturbed; the body is capable of performing its functions, being not yet sunk (*baptized*);" that is, not yet entirely drunk.

Philo Judæus, vol. ii. p. 478—"I know some who, when they easily become intoxicated, before they are entirely sunk (*baptized*)," &c. Philo is another witness to the meaning of *Baptizo* in the time of the Apostles; for he was contemporary with them, and, like them, a Jewish Greek writer.

Athenœus, Deipnos. vii. 37, quotes an ancient author, who says of a drunken man:—" He is drowned or sunk (*baptized*) now the fourth day, leading the life of a miserable mullet."*

Basil, Hom. xiv. p. 491, speaking of the intemperate, says:—" They are more miserable than those who perish in the sea, whom the waves, which are perpetually submerging them, (*baptizing them*,) will not permit to rise; so indeed the souls of these are submerged and carried away, being sunk (*baptized*) with wine."

Chrysostom, Id. Hom. v. on Titus.—" Strange! how were we plunged (*baptized*) in wickedness, so that we could not be purified, but needed a new birth!"

Pindar, Pyth. ii. 139, describing the impotent malice of his enemies, compares himself to the cork on a net in the sea, which on account of its buoyancy will not sink. He says:—" As when a net is cast into the sea, the cork swims above, so I am unsunk (*unbaptized*)."

Plutarch, Moral Galb, speaks of Otho as being "im-

* So Shakspeare—(Tim. of Athens, Act 3, Sc. 5.)
"He has a sin that often
Drowns him."—Viz: Drunkenness.

mersed (*baptized*) in debts of fifty myriads;" that is, not "overwhelmed," as Prof. Stuart renders it, but plunged in debts. "To plunge in debt" is a metaphor we use every day. How would "*sprinkled*" or "*poured in debt*" sound?

Aquila, in Job, ix. 31:—"Thou shalt plunge (*baptize*) me in the mire, and mine own clothes shall abhor me." How would sprinkle or pour, or even wash, sound here?

Symmachus, in Ps. lxix. 2, (lxviii. 2:)—"I am plunged (*baptized*) into the mire of the deep, where there is no standing; I am come into the depths of the sea, and the flood has submerged me."

In the Apocrypha Baptizo does not occur in a figurative sense. In the Septuagint it is found once, and then the metaphor is plain. The passage is Isa. xxi. 4, where the prophet, foreseeing the capture of Babylon, and the subjugation of the empire by the Medes and Persians, says: "My heart pants, and iniquity sinks (*baptizes*) me." The figure is the same as that which we employ in all cases when we speak of sinking, or being ready to sink, in view of approaching and terrible calamities. The same idea occurs in Psalm, xxxviii. 4.—"For mine iniquities are gone over my head; as an heavy burden, they are too heavy for me."

Having proceeded thus far, I now propose the following questions to my reader's conscience: Is it possible to doubt what Christ intends when he uses the word *Baptizo?* Is sprinkling, or pouring, *Baptism?* Is it not a fearful thing to alter an ordinance instituted by the Lord Jesus?

As to most persons, they have never examined the subject. They have been blinded by assertions and statements confidently put forth from the press or the pulpit. I can understand the error of such persons; but I confess I almost despair for the truth, when I find learned men, and men whom so many qualities engage us to love and admire, still fighting against God's precept, and employing such arguments as they use. "It means *immerse*," says one, "but the *mode* is of no importance!" as if *the mode* is not the very *thing*. The mode is certainly of no consequence, provided there be an *immersion*. But is *sprinkling*, or *pouring*, a mode of immersing? There is no sort of analogy between this case and the mode of receiving the Lord's Supper, as is sometimes pretended. In the supper Christ commands nothing but receiving the bread and wine. He prescribes nothing as to the posture, or the sort of bread and wine. As to Baptism, the very thing, the only act, he commands, is Immersion.

Another says, "It cannot be immersion, because in some countries water is scarce." As if there were a spot inhabited by man which does not furnish water enough for immersion. Or, if there were such a spot, as if this would be an argument. Why with just as much reason might it be said that, in the supper, *wine* does not mean *wine*, because in some places wine is not made; or because persons may be cast on an island where no wine could be obtained.

A third impiously talks of "*Indelicacy*;" as if any but a most polluted imagination can associate an impure idea with this beautiful institution. Nay, I do not believe that the most debauched minds ever conceived so wicked a thought, until the opposers of baptism furnished them with it. Thousands of men and women bathe together every summer at Cape May and other places on the sea shore, and this is well. But as soon as a convert goes down into the water to obey Jesus, ministers dare to make insinuations as to indecency, and thus supply the infidel with a weapon, which even his hatred to the Gospel never would have suggested.

I will only add, that one of the latest and most prominent of our opponents drops altogether the act, and assures us that *Baptizo* means *purify*. " John was *purifying* at Enon, because there was much water there !" " Then came Jesus unto Jordan to John to be *purified* of him !" " Go teach all nations, *purifying* them in the name," &c. ! " Therefore we are buried with him by *purification !*" " The like figure whereunto *purification* doth now also save us !" The feelings which are in my bosom as I behold these things are grief and humiliation. Would that men so worthy of our esteem and veneration would cease thus to resist the truth ! We love them, and pray for them, but we tremble when we remember the language of God as to him who " adds to" or " takes from the words" of the Bible. It is appalling to think how many receive the sentiments of these authors, and quiet themselves by their assertions. One consolation, however, is left. It is plain, from this last feeble attempt to defend sprinkling and pouring, that the case is becoming desperate ; that God is causing error to culminate, and show itself on an eminence, and thus be exposed before all.

I will conclude this chapter with the subjoined letter of Dr. Anthon, Professor of Languages in Columbia College, New-York, and one of the best Greek scholars in this country. I give the whole correspondence.

No. 1 Bond Street, New-York, March 23, 1843.

PROFESSOR CHARLES ANTHON:

In conversation with Dr. Spring, last evening, he stated that in the original, the word Baptism, which we find in the New Testament, has no definite or distinct meaning—that it means to immerse, sprinkle, pour, and has a variety of other meanings—as much the one as the other; and that every scholar knows it; that it was the only word that could have been selected by our Saviour, having such a variety, as to suit every one's views and purposes. May I ask you if your knowledge of the language from which the word was taken has led you to the same conclusion? And may I beg of you to let the deep interest I take in the subject plead my apology.

I have the honor to be, with great respect,

Most respectfully yours, E. PARMLY.

Columbia College, March 27, 1843.

DR. PARMLY:

My Dear Sir.—There is no authority whatever for the singular remark made by the Rev. Dr. Spring relative to the force of Baptizo. The primary meaning of the word is to dip or immerse; and its secondary meanings, if ever it had any, all refer, in some way or other, to the same leading idea. Sprinkling, &c., are entirely out of the question. I have delayed answering your letter in the hope that you would call and favor me with a visit, when we might talk the matter over at our leisure. I presume, however, that what I have here written will answer your purpose.

Yours truly,   CHARLES ANTHON.

CHAPTER V.

UP to this point I have examined the meaning of Baptizo in the works of uninspired writers. When the Holy Spirit employed the word its import was well known, and there could have been no doubt what was meant. Indeed, the idea of some ecclesiastic, sacred, mystic signification is, as I have already remarked, perfectly absurd. How monstrous to say that the verb meant *immerse*, but as soon as Jesus commands men to be *immersed* it means *sprinkle!* What, however, explodes forever this plea is, that the inspired penmen attach no magical meaning to the word—they employ it just as we do the term immerse.

To show this I begin with the literal use of Baptizo in the New Testament, when it is not applied to the ordinance. The first case is Mark, vii. 3, 4: "For the

Pharisees and all the Jews except they wash (*Nipsontai*) their hands oft eat not, holding the tradition of the Elders. And when they return from the market, except they wash (*Baptizontai*) they eat not." Now, here are two ablutions. One common and frequent ("*oft*,") the other only on special occasions. The former is expressed by the Greek word *Nipto*, to wash. The latter, of course, is a more thorough purification, and what is the word used? It is *Baptizo*. On this passage I make the following remarks:

In the first place, it has always been a common custom in the East for men, returning from their business, to bathe before dinner.

In the next place, the Evangelist is speaking of the superstitious punctiliousness of the Pharisees. Even when they remain at home they eat not except they washed their hands. Whenever they returned from market, where they may have touched a dead body, they baptized, viz: immersed or bathed before eating.

Mr. Bruce informs us that in Abyssinia the sect called Kemmont "wash themselves from head to foot after coming from the market, or any public place, where they may have touched any one of a different sect from their own, esteeming all such unclean." Is it strange, then, to find the superstitious Pharisees immersing themselves for purification on coming from market?

Dr. G. Campbell, on Mark, vii. 3, 4 :—" For illustrating this passage, let it be observed, first, that the two verbs rendered wash in the English translation, are different in the original. The first is *Nipsontai*, properly translated *Wash;* the second is *Baptizontai*, which limits us to a particular mode of washing; for *Baptizo* denotes *to plunge, to dip.*

Vatablus, a distinguished Professor of Hebrew, at Paris, on Mark, vii. 4, says: "They bathed their whole persons."

Grotius, on Mark, vii. 4 :—" They cleansed themselves more carefully from defilement contracted at the market, to wit, by not only washing their hands, but even by immersing their body."

Maimonides.—" If the Pharisees touched but the garments of the common people they were defiled, all one as if they had touched a profluvious person, and needed immersion; and were obliged to it; hence, when they walked the streets they walked on the side of the way, that they might not be defiled by touching the common people." "In a laver (they say) which holds forty seahs of water, every defiled man dips himself."*

McKnight also, (not only in his Epistles, but in his Harmony of the four Gospels, on Mark, vii. 4,) says: " For when they come from market, except they dip themselves, they eat not."

Indeed, Maimonides (see Lightfoot on Matt. iii. 6,) says: "Wherever, in their law washing of the body or garments is mentioned, it means nothing else than the washing of the whole body. For if any wash himself

* Maim. in Misn. Chagiga, c. 2, sect. 7. See, also, in Hilch Abot Tumaot, c. 13, sect. 8. And again, in Hilch Mikvaot, c. 9, sect. 5.

all over, except the very top of his little finger, he is still in his uncleanness."

Some learned men have thought that the immersion was only of the hands. As far as my argument is concerned, it matters not whether it were the hands, or the whole person. I believe it was the whole person; but it may be as well to give the opinions of some of the learned on this point. Dr. George Campbell thus renders the passage: "For the Pharisees, and indeed all the Jews, observing the traditions of the elders, eat not until they have washed their hands by pouring a little water upon them; and if they come from market, by dipping them."

Buxtorf.—"They taught that, if a person had not departed from the house, the hands, without the fingers being distended, should be wet with water poured over them, and then elevated so that the water might flow down to the elbows." "On the contrary, those who had departed from the house, washed in a bath, or at least, immersed their hands in water with the fingers distended. The ceremony in this case (Mark, vii. 4) is denominated *baptizing* (except they *immerse or bathe*.")
Buxtorf's Chal. Talm. and Rabb. Lexicon, Col. 1335, and Col. 840.

Wetstein (quoted by Dr. Campbell on Mark, vii. 4)— "*Baptizo* here is, to immerse the hands in water. *Nipto*, to pour water on the hands." On this, Dr. Campbell says: "This is more especially the import, when the words are, as here, opposed to each other."

Rosenmuller (in his notes on this passage) speaks of

two modes of washing the hands, namely immersion of the hands in water, and when one hand is washed by the other.

Kuinol (on Mark, vii. 4,) after saying that some thought an immersion of the whole person was meant, says: "But an immersion of the hands, duly performed, would have abundantly sufficed for this end."

Spencer (on the Ritual Laws of the Hebrews) says: "Some of the Jews, ambitious for the credit of superior purity, frequently immersed their whole person in water; the greater part, however, following a milder discipline, frequently washed only their hands, when they were about to take food. That the greater part, and especially the Pharisees, attended to this rite privately at home, and considered it a very important part of religion, is sufficiently evident from Mark, vii. 3, 4. Hence it was that stone vessels for water [water pots, John, ii. 6] were provided in every house of the Hebrews; so that all, when about to take food, might perform the frequent washings according to the discipline of the Pharisees. These vessels were very suitable for performing these daily purifications of the Jews. For it was customary among the Jews, sometimes to wash the hands by water poured upon them; at other times, to immerse the hands in water up to the wrist.

Lastly, Lightfoot says (on Mark, vii. 4:) "The Jews used the washing of hands, and the plunging of the hands. The word *Nipsontai*, wash, in our Evangelist, seems to answer to the former; and *Baptizontai*, to the latter. Those that remain at home, eat not unless they

58 THE ACT OF BAPTISM.

wash first. But those that come from the market eat not, unless they plunge their fist into the water, being ignorant and uncertain what uncleanness they came near unto in the market." The phrase, therefore, (Lightfoot thinks,) " seems to be meant of the immersion or plunging of the hands only."

If to any of my readers I seem to be overloading this treatise with authorities for a plain thing, let them remember that the case demands it. To any man it ought to be enough, that I have proved the only meaning of *Baptizo* to be immerse, and that the Bible says the Pharisees immersed. But, in this controversy, it really seems that the word of God will not be received unless corroborated by human testimony.

The ample quotations just made supersede the necessity of argument on the next passage in which the word *Baptizo* occurs, without reference to the ordinance, viz: Luke, xi. 38. It reads thus: " And when the Pharisee saw it, he marvelled that he had not first washed (*baptized*) before dinner." From the context it appears, that the Saviour had been with a crowd of common and diseased people. The scrupulosity of the Pharisee required, in such a case, the uncommon purification before eating. He, therefore, wondered that Christ did not baptize, i. e. bathe, (either wholly, or his hands,) before dinner. In reply, Jesus rebukes this outward washing, while the heart was still impure. "And the Lord said unto him, Now do ye Pharisees make clean the outside of the cup and the platter, but your inward part is full of ravening and wickedness."

THE ACT OF BAPTISM. 59

Scaliger.—The more superstitious part of them (the Jews) every day, before they sat down to meat, dipped the whole body. Hence the Pharisee's admiration at Christ, Luke, xi. 38.*

The next examples are from Mark, vii. 8th and 4th. "The washing (*baptism*) of pots and cups." "The washing (*baptism*) of cups and pots, brazen vessels, and of tables." As to these the following remarks are conclusive.

First, we have just shown that, in the context, *Baptizo* is applied to the bathing before dinner, and means *immerse*. Secondly, as to the cups, pots (Greek *Xestes*, a pitcher holding a pint and a half) and brazen vessels, there surely is no doubt as to the manner of washing these. In Levit. xi. 32, it is written, "Whatsoever vessel it be wherein any work is done, it must *be put into water*." As to the custom of the Pharisees, of which the text speaks, Maimonides says: "They dip all unclean vessels." "All such vessels were to be immersed before being used." "He that buys a vessel for the use of a feast, of Gentiles, whether molten vessels or glass, they dip them in waters of the laver, and after that may eat and drink in them."†

The difficulty, urged by our opponents, is as to the tables; but this is just as plain as the rest of the passage. *Baptizo*, we have seen, means *immerse*. If it ever meant *sprinkle* or *pour*, it would sometimes be applied to things not capable of immersion. This how-

---

* De Emend. Templ. L. vi. p. 771.

† Maim. Hilch Mik. c. 9. Hilch Maacolot As. c. 17.

ever, is never the case; and in the instance before us there is no room even for a cavil. When tables are mentioned, we think of our massive mahogany furniture, but the Jewish tables are very different. Jahn says (Arch. ch. ix.) "The table in the East, is a piece of round leather, spread upon the floor, upon which is placed a sort of stool. This supports nothing but a platter. The seat was the floor, spread with a mattrass, carpet, or cushion, upon which those who ate sat with legs bent and crossed. They sat in a circle round the piece of leather, with the right side towards the table, so that one might be said to lean upon the bosom of another."

Now, suppose we knew nothing of the superstitious customs of which the Evangelist speaks, would it not be enough that he declares that they immersed these tables? But we do know something of these customs, and we know that tables were defiled, and were cleansed by immersion. "Every vessel of wood, which is made for the use of men, as a table, a bed, receives defilement."* "And these were washed by covering them in water; and very nice they were in washing them, that the water might reach every part, and that they might be covered all over; that there might be nothing which might separate between them and the water and hinder its coming to them; as, for instance, pitch being upon a table, whether within or without, divided between that and the water; and when this was the case it was not rightly washed."†

* Maim. Hilch. Celim. c. 4. † Mism. Mikvaot. c. 9.

Finding all plain as to tables, our opponents contend that the noun translated "*tables,*" means *beds*. I don't care what it means. The Bible says they immersed the articles, and this is enough. But where is the difficulty as to beds? This word, again, suggests to us our heavy furniture; but the couches in the days of Christ were so light, that we find him saying to a man whom he had healed, "Take up thy bed and walk." Heavy or light, however, we have already seen that they were defiled, and the following authority shows that they were immersed. "A bed that is wholly defiled, if he dip it part by part it is pure."* "If he dip the bed in it," (the pool of water) "although its feet are plunged in thick clay" (at the bottom of the pool) "it is clean."†

Dr. Gill (Mark, vii.) has amassed an amount of learning on this point which will satisfy the most critical. The quotations above are sufficient to dissipate all doubt even from a mind so sceptical that it will not credit the Greek language, nor the inspired writer.

Until we come to the ordinance there is only one more instance of the literal use of the term whose import we are examining. In Heb. ix. 10, we read, "Only in meats, and drinks, and divers washings (*baptisms.*") But, after the preceding investigation, I cannot think that this case requires any discussion. We have seen that the Jews practised divers immersions. They immersed themselves on various occasions, and immersed various articles. The books of Leviticus and Numbers

---

* Maim. Hilch. Celim. c. 26. † Mism. Mikv. c. 7.

specify various cases where immersion was required. Indeed, McKnight (Heb. ix. 10) translates this verse, "divers immersions."

CHAPTER VI.

WE come, now, to those passages in the New Testament where *Baptizo* and *Baptisma* are applied to the ordinance. Let me remind my readers that the Holy Ghost never departs from this phraseology. *Baptizo* is always the word. Can a candid man know this, and have followed me so far, and yet have a doubt as to the act required by Jesus Christ?

In this article my first argument (of itself conclusive) is founded upon the *force of the verb employed*. *Baptizo* was a word as common in the days of Christ as *immerse* is now. I have shown that in classic and Hebrew Greek it meant *immerse* and nothing else. Jesus Christ uses this word. The inspired writers use this word. What did they mean—what could they mean—but immerse?

My second argument is drawn from the *places chosen for baptism*. Look at our Pædobaptist brethren, do they go to rivers or places where there is much water? No. They take a parlor or a church, and a basin of water.

But as soon as you open the Bible you are struck with the fact that baptism was performed in a river, or where there was much water. Matthew says, "The people came and were baptized by John in Jordan;" (Mark says, "in the river Jordan.") "John was baptizing at Enon, near to Salim, because there was much water there." "What need" (such is the concession of Towerson, a Pædobaptist) "would there have been of the Baptist's resorting to great confluxes of water,—were it not that the baptism was to be performed by an immersion? a very little water, as we know it doth with us, sufficing for an effusion or sprinkling." In Booth's Pædobap. Exam. vol. i. p. 209, Ed. 2.

Must there not be some misgivings of conscience when such pleas are advanced, as we sometimes find urged against this last passage? For example, what are we to think of this pretext, that much water was needed, not for baptism, but for the people and their horses to drink! If we were to read, that a miller had selected a certain spot for his mill, because there was much water there, would we consider him sane who affirmed that the water was not for working the mill, but for the accommodation of the people who should come to the mill with their mules and horses?

Nor is the other criticism on this passage at all more respectable. The Greek for "much water," is *Polla Udata*, and the Pædobaptist translators have correctly rendered it "much water." But it is now pretended that the phrase only means "many streams!"

Again I ask, must there not be some mutiny of conscience? First, "*Udor*" never means "*stream.*" It always means "*water.*" The plural "*Udata,*" means "*waters,*" and, of itself, imports a quantity. Thus Byron says:

"Once more upon the waters," &c.

Secondly. An adjective is here added, signifying "*much;*" "*Polla Udata,*" "many waters," "much water." Finally, as if to render doubt impossible, this same inspired writer uses the same words in other places where they are admitted on all hands to mean a large quantity of water. I refer to Rev. i. 15.—"And his voice as the sound of many waters." (*Udatoon Polloon.*) Rev. xiv. 2.—"And I heard a voice from heaven, as the voice of many waters," &c. (*Udatoon Polloon.*) Rev. xix. 6.—"And I heard as it were the voice of a great multitude, and as the voice of many waters." (*Udatoon Polloon.*)

In the Septuagint the words occur frequently, and mean much water. The following quotations will show this:—"He sent from above, he took me; he drew me out of *many waters.*" "Surely in the floods of *many waters*, they shall not come nigh unto him." "Rid me and deliver me out of *many waters.*" "The Lord on high is mightier than the noise of *many waters*, yea, than the waves of the sea." "And when they went, I heard the noise of their wings, as the noise of *many waters*, as the voice of the Almighty." "And behold the glory of the God of Israel came from the way of the east, and his voice was like a noise of *many waters.*"

In all these instances the original is Polla Udata, and

THE ACT OF BAPTISM. 65

the comparison is to the tumult of the sea, or a large body of water.

I grieve to find several writers venturing to assert that the location of Enon is known, and that it is a place of springs! Every now and then some newspaper utters this untruth, and it is multiplied by echoes in every quarter. "From the days of Jerome and Josephus, down to the beginning of 1838," (says the Christian Review, March, 1838,) "neither critics nor travelers have been able to settle this question. Cellarius, Rosenmuller, Raumer, and some others, believe that it lay in Samaria. Bachiene, Michaelis, Busching, Tholuck, &c., would place it in Judea. Lampe and several others maintain that it was on the east side of the Jordan. Lücke believes we are left to conjecture; and says, may it not have been on the borders of Judea and Samaria? Kuinöl, Doddridge, Olshausen, and most of those already mentioned, declare that its real situation is unknown."

The following are Pædobaptist authorities, whose names need only be mentioned:

Doddridge.—"It is exceeding difficult to determine the true situation of this place, about which geographical writers are not at all agreed. We may conclude, however, from ver. 26, that it was on the west side of Jordan, as Bethabara, where John had baptized before, was on the other side. But nothing surely can be more evident than that *Polla Udata*, (many waters,) signifies a large quantity of water, it being sometimes used for the Euphrates. Jer. li. 13. (Septuag.) To which I suppose there may also be an allusion, Rev. xvii. 1. Compare Ezek. xliii. 2; and Rev. i. 15; xiv. 2; xix. 6; where the voice of many waters does plainly signify the roaring of a high sea."

Prof. Olshausen, vol. ii. p. 101, says, "John baptized at Enon, because there was deep water there, convenient for immersing."

De Wette translates the passage, " because there was much water there."

Kuinöl (on the passage,) vol. iii. p. 248, says, "an abundance of water, so much that the human body could easily be immersed in it, according to the mode of baptism as then practised; *Udata* does not signify many *streams*, but an abundance of water, as in Rev. i. 15, and other places." So also Grotius.

My third argument is drawn from what *took place before baptism*. Jesus, and the multitude, went to a river. Philip and the Eunuch "went down both into the water." It is sometimes said, that this last expression means only " went down to the water." Suppose it did, why should a nobleman, traveling with his servants, leave his chariot, and he and the minister go down to the water, only to be sprinkled?

But I protest against this custom among our Pædobaptist brethren, of extolling their own translation to the skies, and then in the next breath condemning it. The English Bible is correct. The very verbs occur in the case of Naaman. "He went down (*Katebe*) and dipped (*Ebaptisato*) himself;" and our brethren do not question what this was. Yet when it is said of the

Eunuch and Philip that they "went down (*Katebesan*) into the water, and Philip baptized him," we are told they only went to the edge, and Philip sprinkled him! The objection is a mere quibble. I do not wish to accumulate criticisms unnecessarily, or I could show that in the very cases urged by our opponents, the preposition here rendered "into," has this meaning and no other. The same inspired writer says, "Jacob went down into (*Katebe eis*) Egypt." (Acts, vii. 15.) Does he mean to the edge of Egypt? In the Septuagint the same words occur in Numb. xvi. 33:—"They and all that appertained to them went down (*Katebesan eis*) alive into the pit." Did they only approach the edge of the pit? Mr. Ewing cites the following case to prove that the phraseology does not always denote entrance into. "Rebekah went down to the well, and filled her pitcher." But this case is conclusive against him. The preposition there is different, it is not "*eis*" but "*epi*."— "Rebekah went down to (Katebe *epi*) the well."

Although it is declared that they "came to a certain water," some writers are such hopeless victims to hydrophobia that they deny the existence of a body of water, and attempt to extort a sophistry from the word "desert." (Acts, viii. 26.) "And the angel of the Lord spake unto Philip, saying, Arise, and go towards the south, unto the way that goeth down from Jerusalem unto Gaza, which is desert." What will not men do who are bent on the support of error? The word "desert" means a solitary place; how can this affect the argument? All critics agree that the geography cannot be exactly fixed.

But that there could not have been water, because the road was unfrequented, or the country uninhabited, is a strange conceit. Bloomfield says, that if the road lay in a direct line, "it must have passed most of the way over a hilly and barren tract, through no town of any note. And, therefore, the epithet *Eremos* ('desert',) which merely means uninhabited, or very thinly peopled, would be suitable enough."

My fourth argument is based upon the declaration of the Scriptures as to *the act performed in baptizing.* "Were baptized of him in (*en*) Jordan." "Were all baptized of him in (*en*) the river Jordan." "Was baptized of John in (*eis*) Jordan." Were they sprinkled, or poured in the river Jordan? But may not the prepositions mean "*at* the Jordan?" Suppose they can; still, would people go to a river to be sprinkled or poured upon? When united with *Baptizo*, however, these prepositions *en* and *eis*, never mean less than "*in*," and "*into*." In the case of Naaman it is "*Ebaptizato en to Jordane;*" and this is admitted to mean "dipped himself in the Jordan." What more can we want, to determine the act performed in the New Testament, where the very words are repeated? As to Mark, i. 9, even Bloomfield confesses the meaning to be conclusive. He says, "*eis* is not here for *en*, as most commentators imagine, who adduce examples which are quite inapposite. The sense of *Ebaptisthe eis* is, was dipped, or plunged into the water."

I here furnish my readers with another morsel from one of the Baltimore tracts. "If it be insisted upon, that the Eunuch was actually immersed, then it proves too much. For nothing is said of the Eunuch that is not said of Philip! They went down both into the water, and when they were come up out of the water." (The writer expunges the words "and he baptized him")!! "If the Eunuch was actually immersed, then Philip was in like manner immersed!!! And if Philip was not immersed, then there is no evidence that the Eunuch was actually immersed!!!! On the principle of correct reasoning this cannot be contradicted"!!!!!*

My fifth and last argument is founded on *what followed baptism.* "Jesus, when he was baptized, went up straightway out of the water."—(Matt. iii. 16.) "And when they" (Philip and the Eunuch) "were come up out of the water." Did they go into the water to be sprinkled? But may not the words rendered "*out of,*" mean only "*from?*" No. When joined to a verb of motion the preposition "*ek,*" used in the case of the Eunuch, never means less than "*out of.*" This case, therefore, is conclusive. In the baptism of Christ the preposition is "*apo,*" and may mean "*from.*" But in the account of the Eunuch it is "*ek,*" which, with a verb of motion, always signifies "*out of.*" Many examples could easily be brought; as Rev. xiii. 1.—"I stood upon the sand of the sea and saw a beast rising up out of (*ek*) the sea." Does this mean "from the edge of the sea?" So Rev. vii. 14.—"These are they which came out of (*ek*) great tribulations." Did they come from the edge of tribula-

* Christian Baptism, by Thomas Lape, A. M., p. 59, Fourth Edition.

tions? No critic will deny that Philip and the Eunuch came from out the water. But they could not come from out the water had they not first gone into it. And if they went into it, the baptism was immersion. I ask any man, what would he think if a minister took a candidate to a body of water, and went into the water with him, for the purpose of sprinkling or pouring?

In the former portions of this essay I established so clearly the signifation of *Baptizo*, that any Greek scholar, who had never seen the New Testament, if told that Jesus commands his disciples to be immersed, would say, "Then he must use the word *Baptizo*." In this chapter the act required is so manifest, that any plain, unprejudiced man, knowing nothing of Greek, when informed that the thing done was in Greek expressed by *Baptizo*, would at once say, "Then I know the meaning of one Greek word; *Baptizo* certainly means *immerse*."

CHAPTER VII.

In this chapter we will take up, in order, the allusions to baptism, which are found in the New Testament.

In Luke, xii. 50, Jesus says: "I have a baptism to be baptized with." Here he speaks of the sufferings which were to overwhelm him. The metaphor is full of energy: "I am about to be plunged in deep affliction." Can a few drops of water sprinkled on the face be any emblem here? Witsius thus renders it: "Immersion into the water, is to be considered by us, as exhibiting that dreadful abyss of Divine justice, in which Christ for our sins, was for a time, as it were, absorbed; as in David, his type, he complains Psalm, lxix. 2, 'I am come into deep waters, where the floods overflow me.'" Œcon. of the Cov. L. iv. c. xvi. § 26.

1 Cor. x. 1, 2.—"Moreover, brethren, I would not that ye should be ignorant, how that all our fathers were under the cloud, and all passed through the sea: And were all baptized unto Moses in the cloud and in the sea." Here the figure is plain. There was neither sprinkling, nor pouring. The Israelites went down into the sea. The waters parted and rose up on each side, as walls; and the cloud, which had stood between the two armies, now moved and covered them. Whitby says: "They were covered with the sea on both sides, Exod. xiv. 22; so that both the cloud and the sea had some resemblance to our being covered with water in baptism. Their going into the sea resembled the ancient rite of going into the water; and their coming out of it, their rising up out of the water."

Professor Stuart says: "As the language must evidently be figurative in some good degree, and not literal, I do not see how, on the whole, we can make less of it, than to suppose that it has a tacit reference to the idea of surrounding in some way or other." "The suggestion has sometimes been made, that the Israelites were sprinkled by the cloud and by the sea, and this was the baptism which Paul meant to designate. But the cloud on this occasion, was not a cloud of rain; nor do we find any intimation that the waters of the Red Sea sprinkled the children of Israel at this time." p. 336.

Witsius.—" How were the Israelites baptized in the cloud, and in the sea, seeing they were neither immersed in the sea, nor wet by the cloud ? It is to be considered that the apostles here uses the term baptism in a figurative sense. The cloud hung over their heads; and so the water is over those that are baptized. The sea surrounded them on each side; and so the water in regard to those that are baptized." Œcon. Fæd. L. iv. c. x. § 11.

Similar to this last passage is 1 Peter, iii. 20, where it is said, that as Noah was saved by water, so, now, baptism figuratively represents that by which we are saved, viz: The death and burial and resurrection of Christ.

The other allusions to baptism are in Rom. vi. 3, 4, 5, and Coloss. ii. 12, " Know ye not that so many of us as were baptized into Jesus Christ were baptized into his death ? Therefore, we are buried with him by baptism into death : that, like as Christ was raised up from the dead by the glory of the Father, even so we also should walk in newness of life. For if we have been planted together in the likeness of his death, we shall be also in the likeness of his resurrection." " Buried with him in baptism, wherein also ye are risen with him through the faith of the operation of God, who hath raised him from the dead." These passages are conclusive.

I am sorry to find Dr. Kurtz affirming that Judson

gives up these passages. He says, "Mr. Robinson, the Baptist historian, and Mr. Judson, the Baptist missionary, who both strenuously maintained the necessity of submersion, admit that this passage is misapplied, when used as evidence of the mode of baptism. Here we have two eminent men, decided advocates of plunging, coinciding in the declaration that this passage affords no proof in favor of their mode of baptism."*

I have not Robinson, but just hear Judson, and tell me if on any other subject men were ever thus unguarded.

"Baptism is, by the Apostle Paul, repeatedly compared to a burial. In one passage believers are said to be buried with Christ by baptism, and in another, to be buried with him in baptism, and to be therein risen with him. Whether baptism in these passages denotes external or spiritual baptism, it is evident that the figure derives all its propriety and beauty from some implied resemblance between the external rite and a burial; nor can it be imagined that the apostles would have ever compared baptism of any kind to a burial, had there been no such resemblance." "We may rest assured that if baptism had consisted in sprinkling or pouring, or any partial application of water whatever, though we might possibly have heard of being washed in baptism, we should never have heard of being buried in baptism; for there being no resemblance between such applications of water and a burial, there could have been no propriety in representing baptism under such a figure. But

* Kurtz on Baptism, p. 244.

there is a confessed resemblance between immersion and a burial; and since the phrase, buried in baptism, is sanctioned by the highest authority, even Divine inspiration, we have invincible proof that baptism consists not in sprinkling or pouring, but in immersion."*

Observe, the apostle expressly says that we are "buried *by baptism*" and "*in baptism.*" He also calls it a "planting." He then adds, that in baptism there is not only a burying, but a "*rising.*" The pretence that a spiritual burial is here meant conflicts directly with the very word of God. That word says "*by*" and "*in*" the act of baptism the subject is buried. The apostle had before spoken of the inward change (see context;) he here speaks of the external baptismal profession of Christ.

As for what is sometimes said about the ancient mode of burying, and the assertion that Christ was not buried, I can hardly think our brethren serious when they write such things. The idea is simply a being covered and hidden. The manner is nothing. With reference to Christ's burial, the apostle says: "Christ was buried and rose again on the third day." And Jesus, alluding to his burial, employs the very idea of the passage before us, "For as Jonas was three days and three nights in the whale's belly, so shall the Son of Man be three days and three nights in the heart of the earth."—Matt. xii. 40.

Bloomfield.—"There is here (Rom. vi. 4) plainly a reference to the ancient mode of baptism by immersion;

---

* Judson on Baptism, p. 18.

and I agree with Koppe and Rosenmuller that there is reason to regret it should have been abandoned in most Christian churches, especially as it has so evident a reference to the mystic sense of baptism."

Rosenmuller (on the passage.)—"Immersion in the water of baptism and coming forth out of it, was a symbol of a person's renouncing his former life, and, on the contrary, beginning a new one. The learned have rightly reminded us that on account of this emblematical meaning of baptism, the rite of immersion ought to have been retained in the Christian church."

Dr. Knapp, an eminent and pious German divine, whose works are recommended by Dr. Woods, speaking of the passage in question, says: "We are, like Christ, buried as dead persons by baptism, and should arise like him, to a new life." "The image is taken here from baptized persons, as they were immerged (buried,) and as they emerged (rose again.")

John Wesley, on Rom. vi. 4.—"Buried with him, alluding to the ancient manner of baptizing by immersion."

Whitby, on Rom. vi. 4, author of a Commentary on the New Testament, and more than forty other learned works.—"It being so expressly declared here, Rom. vi. 4, and Coloss. ii. 12, that we are buried with Christ in baptism by being buried under water; and the argument to oblige us to a conformity to his death, by dying to sin, being taken hence; and this immersion being religiously observed by all Christians for thirteen centuries and approved by our Church, and the change of it into sprinkling, even without any allowance from the author of this institution, or any license from any council of the Church, being that which the Romanist still urges to justify his refusal of the cup to the laity; it were to be wished that this custom might be again of general use, and aspersion only permitted, as of old, in case of the Clinic, or in present danger of death."

Lastly, Archbishop Tillotson.—"Anciently those who were baptized put off their garments, which signified the putting off the body of sin, and were immersed and buried in water to represent their death to sin; and then did rise up out of the water, to signify their entrance upon a new life. And to these customs the apostle alludes when he says: 'How shall we that are dead to sin live any longer therein? Know ye not that so many of us as were baptized into Jesus Christ were baptized into his death? Therefore, we are buried with him by baptism.'" Vol. 1, p. 493.

Chrysostom proves the resurrection from the apostolic mode of baptism. "Our being baptized and immerged in the water, and our rising again out of it, is a symbol of our descending into hell or the grave, and of our returning from them." Chrys. Hom. ii. 1. Cor. p. 689.

Indeed, only try sprinkling or pouring in these passages, and how will it sound? "Know ye not that so many of us as were *poured* into Jesus Christ were *poured* into his death? Therefore we are buried with him by *pouring* into death!" Or let us try "sprinkled." "Know ye not that so many of us as were *sprinkled* into Jesus Christ were *sprinkled* into his death? Therefore we are buried with him by *sprinkling* into death!" It is certain, then, this verse requires immersion. But note, the apostle here declares that all who are baptized are so buried.

CHAPTER VIII.

WHILE writing the last few lines I have received some parts of Baptist Noel's work on Baptism. My readers know that he has long stood at the head of the evangelical party of the Church of England, and has lately joined a Baptist church in London. He says: "During my ministry in the Establishment, *an indefinite fear of the conclusions at which I might arrive, led me to avoid the study of the question of baptism.*" Judson, Jewett, and others, have recorded similar confessions. Shall I be accused of uncharitableness when, with the foregoing mass of testimony before me, I say, that multitudes are unconvinced because they are unwilling to look at the subject? I have already stated some of the pleas which have been brought to the defense of the degenerate rite now practised instead of baptism. In this chapter I will state others.

"How could the 3,000 be baptized in one day?" To this I have two answers. First, it is no where said that they were baptized in one day. The historian only informs us, that there was an accession of 3,000. "Then they that gladly received the word were baptized. And the same day there was added unto them about three thousand souls." Acts, xii. 14.

But there would have been no sort of difficulty in baptizing more than 3,000 in a part of a day. The twelve apostles, and the seventy, besides others, were on the spot. Each administrator would thus have only a few candidates. I have, myself, on more than one occasion, baptized between one and two hundred, and it occupied a very short time. This objection supposes that none but the apostles baptized, which is manifestly an error. In the case of Cornelius and his friends, Peter "commanded them to be baptized." Paul tells us that he baptized only a few. He adds, "Christ sent me not to baptize" (viz: any body can do that) "but to preach the Gospel." 1 Cor. i. 17.

On this question facts are the shortest argument, and we have historical facts directly to the point. Upon Easter Sunday, April 16, 404, Chrysostom, aided by the clergy of his own church, did immerse about 3,000 Catechumens. This took place at Constantinople. An enraged rabble of soldiers twice interrupted the ordinance, yet it was easily performed. (Chrysost. Ep. ad Innoc. v. 3, 518.) Again, in 496, Remigus, bishop of Rheims, immersed Clovis and three thousand of his subjects. Of course he was aided by his presbyters. (Schröckh's Church History, vol. xvi. p. 234.)*

---

* Dr. Kurtz goes into the matter arithmetically. He declares that the apostles alone had the prerogative of baptizing! Then he assures us that it requires five or six minutes to immerse one

THE ACT OF BAPTISM. 79

"But where could they find water for 3,000?" Was there ever such insatiable scepticism? Is God's truth thus to be contested inch by inch? If we were to receive news that at Maulmain our missionaries had baptized 3,000, would any one question the statement on candidate!! We are next informed as to the precise hour when the apostles began. "They began at one o'clock, or probably later"!!! Lastly, he keeps them in the water through the remainder of the day, and "until four minutes after five the next day"!!!! No wonder our brethren are in consternation, and bestir themselves tremulously against this amphibious life.— Every Baptist minister knows that baptizing is not laborious. It requires scarcely any effort, and is most delightfully refreshing. Would to God that Dr. Kurtz, and three thousand other pious men in this place, would do their duty to Christ, and be baptized. I promise them they shall be detained at the Spring Gardens not more than a few hours, and that I will find administrators enough to undertake and survive the formidable achievement. In Baptisteries more time is consumed, but when candidates enter a river in companies, two are easily baptized in a minute. I have more than once thus baptized between one and two hundred before morning service on the Sabbath. The twelve apostles would not have required more than two hours and a half. If the seventy assisted, the 3,000 could have been baptized in less than 25 minutes. Dr. Miller is terrified at the very thought of immersing. He pronounces it "one of the most severe and exhausting efforts to human strength that can well be undertaken," and pleads the age and infirmity of some ministers as an argument against it. Dr. Kurtz has caught the panic from Dr. Miller. Both of them quote with evident concern and dismay, the following appalling statement: "a gentleman of veracity told the writer, that he was once present when forty-seven were dipped in one day, in the usual way. The first operator began and went through the ceremony until he had dipped twenty-five the ground that the missionaries could not find water? Yet thus it is when the Bible declares a fact.

If there was water for one hundred, why not for three thousand? Besides, of all inland cities, Jerusalem is the last where there could have been any scarcity of water. In his work on **Palestine**, Robinson spends nineteen pages speaking of the various and exuberant supplies of water.

Though often besieged and suffering greatly from famine, we never find a want of water in this city. Nor is this surprising, for Jerusalem was the capital of Judea, "a land of brooks of water, of fountains and depths that spring out of valleys and hills," (Deut. viii. 7.) The 3,000 were baptized at Pentecost, when a vast concourse of Jews assembled in the metropolis, required ample accommodations for the daily immersions which they practiced. Close by the city was the stream Cedron, which, at this season, (Spring,) would furnish abundant water. There were other streams to the south of Jerusalem, flowing from the fountains of Siloam and Gihon. Private reservoirs and pools for bathing were so common, that

persons; when he was so fatigued, that he was compelled to give it up to the other, who with great apparent difficulty dipped the other twenty-two. Both appeared completely exhausted, and went off the ground into a house hard by to change their clothes, and refresh themselves." (Scripture Directory for Baptism, by a Layman, 14.) Mr Lape is more venturesome and chivalrous; his fears are not for himself, but for the ladies. "Who will deny," he exclaims, "but that severe sickness, derangement, and even death have not oftentimes been the sad consequences of their immersion."

cistern-digging was one of the trades of the laboring classes; and out of the 3,000, many must have owned these reservoirs, and would gladly invite the apostles to use them. Lastly, in and around the city were several reservoirs, (or "swimming places," as the Greek word calls them,) built for the public use.

One of these was Bethesda, which Maundrel, the traveler, describes as being 120 paces long, 40 wide, and 8 feet deep. Then, there was Struthius, mentioned by Josephus (Bell, c. v. xi. 4.) Then, there was the Lower Pool by the Fish Gate (Is. xxii. 9.) Then, there was the Upper Pool (Is. vii. 3.) To the southeast was Siloam, mentioned, John, ix. 7. These, and other places, were all convenient, and supplied accommodation for the immersion of any number of persons.

A second objection has been urged. It is the difficulty of baptizing the jailor and his household (Acts xvi.) And to this I have two answers.

The immersion of criminals in jails, has often occurred in this country. When the papers have stated that, "at such a place the Baptist minister immersed a criminal in the prison," nobody ever doubts the fact. It is only when the Bible affirms anything, it at once becomes incredible. In the East every house had abundant accommodations for bathing; and if the sacred writer had given no intimation as to the place of the jailor's baptism, this cavil would have been perfectly idle. Dr. Judson, preaching at Calcutta, says, "This case (that of the jailor) can present no difficulty to the minds of any of you, who may have been within the yard of the prison in this city, or are acquainted with the fact, that prison yards, in the East, as well as yards and gardens of private houses, are usually furnished with tanks of water."

While, however, the baptism might have been in the jail, I think it was not. From the account, they were baptized at some spot away from the house,* probably at the river mentioned in verse 13. The history shows that the jailor and his family resided in the jail. So it is clear, from v. 34, that they went out for baptism. In v. 32, the apostles "spake the word to him and to all that were in his house." Then follows the baptism, (v. 33,) for which they went out, since, *after the baptism*, they returned to the house. "When he had brought them into his house he set meat before them." (v. 34.) This case shows the importance attached, by the apostles, to baptism; for although it was night, yet baptism was at once administered. If ever there could be an instance where one ought to wait, it was this; yet see what a precedent God has set us here.

There is only one more argument urged by our opponents. It is the figurative use of Baptizo with reference to the Holy Spirit; and as this has misled many people, it deserves some attention.

In Matt. iii. 11, it is said, by John, "I baptize you with water, but he that cometh after me shall baptize you with the Holy Ghost and with fire." The seeming difficulty here vanishes, when I mention that the Greek

---

* So abundantly irrigated was the spot occupied by Philippi, that the city was called by its founders, Crenedes (Greek, Crene, a spring.)

is, *en*, "*in water*," and "*in the Holy Ghost and in fire.*" Indeed, we have already shown that John baptized, not with the Jordan, but in it; and as the same preposition is here applied to the spiritual baptism, there can be no doubt of its meaning.

The expression is figurative, and alludes to the copious communications of the Holy Spirit. The figure is precisely like those cited in ch. iv., where persons are said to be immersed in wine, &c. Sprinkling or pouring a little water, of course, is not the idea. Prof. Robinson translates the passage thus: "He shall baptize you in the Holy Ghost and in fire." When used with Baptizo the preposition *en* has always the sense of in or into. Naaman "dipped himself in (*en*) the Jordan." "Were baptized in (*en*) the river Jordan." "I baptize you in (*en*) water, but he that cometh after me shall baptize you in (*en*) the Holy Ghost and in (*en*) fire." The meaning cannot be mistaken. It is this: So abundant shall be the influences of the Holy Spirit, that you shall be bathed in them. "Holy Spirit and fire" is a Greek idiom for "the fire of the Holy Spirit." It is like Luke xxi. 15, "A mouth and wisdom," for the wisdom of speech." So in 1 Kings, xix. 12, the original is, "stillness and a voice," for "a still voice."

The verse, then, is a prediction that Jesus would immerse his people in the illuminating and purifying influences of the Holy Ghost. The Greek fathers, who best understood the Greek, so render it.

Theophylact, commenting on the words, says: "That is, he shall inundate you abundantly with the gifts of the

Spirit." Cyril of Jerusalem, Cateches. xvii. 8.—"For as he that goes down into the water and is baptized is surrounded on all sides by the water, so the apostles were totally baptized (immersed) by the Spirit. The water surrounds the body externally, but the Spirit incomprehensibly baptizes (immerses) the soul within."

"But is not the Spirit said to be "*poured?*" What, then? Does this prove that Baptizo means pour? As well might it be argued that Baptizo means to fly, because the Spirit is said to " descend like a dove ;" or that it signifies to *blow*, because Christ compares the Spirit's operations to the blowing of the wind As our opponents often perplex people's minds by this metaphor, I beg my reader to attend to the following remarks:

First, we have shown that the literal import of *Baptizo* is to immerse; and the figurative use of the word must, of course, retain the same idea.

Secondly, when the Holy Spirit is said to be " poured," what are we to understand? The Holy Spirit is a Divine Being. A Divine Being cannot be poured; and all feel that the expression is figurative. As the Spirit is supposed to dwell in heaven, his influences will be spoken of as coming down. In the gospel dispensation God promises not a distilling only, but an abundant effusion of these influences. Peter says : " He hath saved us by the washing of regeneration, and renewing of the Holy Ghost, which he shed on us abundantly."

Let us go on. The Spirit is poured down, and in such glorious abundance, that we are figuratively declared to be baptized or immersed in it. *Baptizo* not only does

THE ACT OF BAPTISM. 85

not mean pour, but it is self-evident that it means a different action. To put this in a plain light, let me ask what is done when I baptize on Sabbath evenings? First, the water is poured into the baptistery. Is this baptism? No. The baptism follows: when an abundance of water having fallen into the font, the candidate is immersed.

On the day of Pentecost there was a literal baptism in the Spirit. Jesus compares the Spirit to the *wind*. On that day "suddenly there came a sound from heaven as of a rushing mighty *wind*, and it filled all the house where they were sitting;" "and they were all filled with the Holy Ghost." But the pouring of the Spirit, and baptizing in the Spirit, are figurative expressions. They are like this passage in English, "The sun poured his effulgence on the landscape, and bathed the mountain in light." How absurd here to say that *bathe* means *pour*. The same explanation applies to cases where the Holy Ghost is said to "fall." In Acts, xi. 15, 16, there is a reference to such an abundant stream of divine influence, that the persons are figuratively said to be immersed in it. Peter says: "And as I began to speak, the Holy Ghost fell on them, as on us at the beginning. Then remembered I the word of the Lord, how that he said, John indeed baptized with water, but ye shall be baptized with the Holy Ghost." In the original it is, "John indeed baptized in water, but ye shall be baptized in the Holy Ghost." This was a Pentecostal season with the Gentiles. We have already seen that on the day of Pentecost there was a literal immersion of Jews. Peter here declares that the same thing took place on this occasion with Gentiles. The following are comments of eminent Pædobaptist writers. I copy them from Booth's reply to Williams.

Gurtlerus.—"Baptism in the Holy Spirit is immersion into the pure waters of the Holy Spirit, or a rich and abundant communication of his gifts. For he on whom the Holy Spirit is poured out, is as it were immersed into him."

Bp. Reynolds.—"The Spirit, under the gospel, is compared to water; and that not a little measure, to sprinkle or bedew, but to baptize the faithful in, (Matt. iii. 2, Acts, i. 5,) and that not in a font or vessel, which grows less and less, but in a spring or living river."

Ikenius.—"The Greek word Baptismos denotes the immersion of a thing or person into something. Here, also, (Matt. iii. 11, compared with Luke, iii. 16,) the baptism of fire, or that which is performed in fire, must signify, according to the same simplicity of the letter, an immission or immersion into fire; and this the rather because here to baptize in the Spirit and in fire, are not only connected, but also opposed to being baptized in water."

Le Clerc.—"He shall baptize you in the Holy Spirit. As I plunge you in water, he shall plunge you, so to speak, in the Holy Spirit."

Casaubon.—"To baptize is to immerse, and in this sense the apostles are truly said to be baptized; for the house in which this was done was filled with the Holy Ghost, so that the apostles seemed to be plunged into it as into a fish-pool."

Abp. Tillotson.—"It (the sound from heaven, Acts, ii. 2) filled all the house. This is that which our Saviour calls baptizing with the Holy Ghost. So that they who sat in the house were, as it were, immersed in the Holy Ghost, as they who were buried with water, were overwhelmed and covered all over with water, which is the proper notion of baptism."

Bp. Hopkins.—"Those that are baptized with the Spirit, are, as it were, plunged into that heavenly flame whose searching energy devours all their dross, tin, and base alloy."

CHAPTER IX.

In inquiring into the import of a Greek word, the following questions must at once suggest themselves to the mind of every man:—Is the Greek language now spoken by any nation? If it be, why not refer the point to them, since they must know what is the meaning of the word?

Now, the Greek language is still essentially a living language. The word *Baptizo* is still used by the Greeks, and they mock to utter scorn the absurdity of supposing that it means sprinkle, or pour. They employ terms of contempt for those practices, and always immerse any members who join their churches from other churches where they have only received sprinkling or pouring. This point is conceded by all, but I add the subjoined authorities.

Professor Stuart ("The Mode of Baptism," p. 76) says: "The mode of baptism by immersion, the Oriental Church has always continued to preserve even down to the present time. The members of this Church are accustomed to call the members of the Western Churches, "sprinkled Christians," by way of ridicule and contempt. They maintain that Baptizo can mean nothing but immerge, and that baptism by sprinkling is as great a solecism as immersion by sprinkling; and they claim to themselves the honor of having preserved the ancient sacred rite of the Church free from change and corruption, which would destroy its significancy."

Augusti, vol. xii. p. 226.—"The Oriental Church has not only preserved unchanged the custom of immersion, but declares it so essential that they re-baptize those who were sprinkled, and by way of contempt call them 'sprinkled Christians.'"

Walch (History of Religious Controversies, vol. v. p. 476) says: "The Greeks not only immerse the candidate thrice under water, so that the water closes over his head, but consider that such a mode of baptism is essential. They reject sprinkling."

Dr. Wall (History of Infant Baptism, vol. ii. p. 376, ed. 3.)—"The Greek Church, in all the branches of it, does still use immersion."

Dr. Knapp (Professor of Theology in the University

THE ACT OF BAPTISM. 89

of Halle) says: "In the Greek Church they still hold to immersion. It would have been better to have adhered generally to the ancient practice, even as Luther and Calvin allowed." (New York Ed. 1848, p. 486.)

Stourtza, a native Greek, (in a work published in 1816,) says: "Baptizo has but one signification. It signifies, literally and invariably, to plunge."

The Greek Patriarch, Jeremiah.—"The ancients were not accustomed to sprinkle the candidate, but to immerse him." (Walch's Controversies out of the Lutheran Church, vol. v. p. 477.)

Christopulos, a Greek, in his "Confession of Faith," C. 7, says: "We follow the example of the apostles, who immersed the candidate under the water."

The great standard of the Greek Church is The Pedalion, (The Helm,) duly authenticated by the Patriarch and Holy Synod. At pp. 29–33, the Pedalion speaks thus: "We say that the baptism of the Latins" (Roman Catholics) "is baptism falsely named" (*Pseudonumon Baptisma*.) Again, "The Latins are heretics of old, specially from the very fact that they are unbaptized" (*Abaptistoi*.) Again, "The more ancient Latins, the first to make innovations upon apostolic baptism, practised pouring, (*Epikusin*,) that is, they poured a little water upon the crown of the child's head. And this is still practised in some places at the present time. More, however, now, with a bunch of hog's bristles throw a few drops of water thrice upon the child's forehead." Again, "Observe, then, that we do not say that we re-baptize (*Anabaptizomen*) the Latins, but that we

6

baptize (*Baptizomen*) them, since their baptism (baptisma) is a lie in its very name." "It is not baptism at all, but bare sprinkling" (Rantisma.)

A celebrated treatise, authenticated by the Patriarchs of Jerusalem, Constantinople, and Alexandria, is called *Rantismou Steleteusis* (an exposure of sprinkling.) Here are the titles of some of the chapters.

Title of chapter vii.—"A Demonstration that Sprinkling is not Ancient, and that the Proofs adduced by Papists are Lies."

Title of chapter viii.—"Reproofs of the Fathers against Sprinkling."

Title of chapter xiv.—"A Demonstration that the Law of the Church to admit the Latins as Baptized was made when they were accustomed to Baptize as we do. Also Witnesses from Latin Authors that Sprinkling was not then received by them."

Title of chapter xix.—"A Demonstration that Baptism is the command of the Lord; Sprinkling that of Satan."

Title of chapter xxvi.—"A Demonstration that Sprinkling, being Satanical, is opposed to Divine Baptism."

Title of chapter xxxiv.—"A Demonstration that Sprinkling, being a Heretical Dogma, is under Anathema."

CHAPTER X.

In this chapter I will glance at the history of Baptism, and indicate the origin and progress of that change which has abolished the institution of Jesus Christ, and substituted a supposititious rite in its place.

Even in the days of the apostles we find corruptions insinuating themselves. Scarcely had Paul left Corinth, before the Lord's Supper was changed into a bacchanalian revelry. Very soon after the time of the apostles all manner of innovations and abuses began to creep in, until the present practices of the Church of Rome were introduced and consolidated.

As to baptism, I have already shown that, in the apostolic age, it was immersion. The Greek Church, notwithstanding its multiplied aberrations from the simplicity of the gospel, still, to this day, practises only immersion. Upon this, as we have seen, that Church prides itself. There is, however, no merit in this seeming fidelity to the truth. It is fidelity, not to Christ, but to the Greek language. The Greeks could no more suppose that *Baptizo* means to sprinkle, or pour, than we could think that to *immerse* is to pour, or sprinkle.

For several centuries, immersion alone was practised by all the churches. Professor Stuart, after many quotations to show this, closes with the following remarkable concession. "But enough. 'It is,' says Augusti, (Denkiv. vii. p. 216,) 'a thing made out,' viz, the ancient practice of immersion. So indeed all the writers who have thoroughly investigated this subject, conclude. I know of no one usage of ancient times, which seems to be more clearly and certainly made out. I cannot see how it is possible for any candid man, who examines the subject, to deny this." (p. 359.) He also, p. 361, gives the following from Brenner. "Thirteen hundred years was baptism generally and ordinarily performed by the immersion of a man under water; and only in extraordinary cases was sprinkling or effusion permitted. These latter methods of baptism were called in question, and even prohibited."

The following authorities furnish an authentic record on this subject. They show how a degenerate theology first contrived and then sanctioned that degenerate rite which has almost superseded baptism.

Barnabas, (supposed to have been contemporary with the apostles,) Ep. c. ii. says: "We descend into the water and come out of it."

Hermas, (supposed to have been contemporary with the apostles,) Pastor, 3.—"Men descend into the water bound to death, but ascend out of it sealed to life." Augusti, vii. 77, after quoting the passage at length, adds: "This passage contains distinct evidence of the custom of immersion."

Justin Martyr, A. D. 140—1, Apol. 61, in giving the Emperor a full account of Christian doctrines and practices, says:—"Those who believe are led to some place where there is water," "and are washed in the water."

Tertullian, A. D. 200, —De Bap., says:—"We are immersed in water," (*mergimer*, in another passage, *mergitamur*,) " let down into the water and dipped" (*tinctus*.) " Peter immersed (*tinxit*) in the Tiber." " It is one thing to be sprinkled (*aspergi*) by the violence of the waves in a boat, and another to be dipped (*tingeri*) in a religious ordinance." " It is indifferent whether one is baptized in the sea or in a pool, in a river or fountain, in a lake or the bed of a river." The flood he calls, " the baptism of the world."

Apostolic Constitutions, 3d Century, Lib. 3, c. 17.— "Baptism relates to the death of Christ; the water answers to the grave; the immersion represents our dying with him; the emersion our rising with him."

Clement of Alexandria, 3d Century, Mystagog. 2.— " You were led to a bath, as Christ was conveyed to the sepulchre, and were thrice immersed, to signify Christ's three days' burial."

Cyril of Jerusalem, (3d Century,) Cat. 17.—" He who is immersed in water and baptized, is surrounded with water on all sides." And. Cat. Mystag. 2.—" As in the night, so in immersion, as if it were night, you can see nothing."

Basil the Great, (4th Century,) De Spiritu Sancto, 15.—" By three immersions we represent the death of Christ ;"—" the bodies of those that are baptized are, as it were, buried in water."

Gregory Nyssen, (4th Century,) De Bap. Christi.— " Coming to the water we conceal ourselves in it, as the Saviour concealed himself in the earth." And Orat. Cat. 35.—" Being thrice overwhelmed in the water, and again raised from it, we imitate the burial and resurrection of Christ." Again: "All the dead are buried under ground, instead of which, water is used in baptism."

Chrysostom, (4th Century,) 25 Hom. on John.—"When our heads enter the water, as a tomb, the old man is buried, and plunging down is wholly concealed all at once."

Augustine (4th Century.)—"After you professed your belief three times did we submerge (*demersemus*) your heads in the sacred fountain."

Theodoret (5th Century,) on Rom. vi. 4.—"Baptism is a type of our Lord's death;" and on Heb. vi. 2.—"In holy baptism we receive the type of the resurrection."

The following quotations are from eminent Pædobaptist authors, who concede the point.

Mr. Chambers.—"In the primitive times, this ceremony was performed by immersion; as it is to this day, in the Oriental Churches, according to the original signification of the word."*

Dr. Wall.—" We should not know by these accounts, (John, iii. 23; Mark, i. 5; Acts, viii. 38,) whether the whole body of the baptized was put under water, head and all, were it not for two later proofs, which seem to me to put it out of the question. One, that St. Paul does twice, in an allusive way of speaking, call baptism a burial, which allusion is not so proper, if we conceive them to have gone into the water, only up to the armpits, &c. as it is, if their whole body was immersed. The other, the custom of the near succeeding times.

* Cyclopædia, Art. Baptism, Edit. 7th.

THE ACT OF BAPTISM. 95

As for sprinkling, I say, as Mr. Blake, at its first coming up in England, 'Let them defend it that use it.'"*

Bingham.—"There are a great many passages in the Epistle of St. Paul, which plainly refer to this custom (immersion.) As this was the original apostolical practice, so it continued to be the universal practice of the church, for many ages, upon the same symbolical reasons, as it was first used by the apostles."†

Dr. Towerson.—"But, therefore, as there is so much the more reason to represent the rite of immersion as the only legitimate right of baptism, because the only one that can answer the ends of its institution, and those things which were to be signified by it; so especially, if (as is well known, and undoubtedly of great force) the general practice of the primitive church was agreeable thereto, and the practice of the Greek Church to this very day. For who can think, either the one, or the other, would have been so tenacious of so troublesome a rite, were it not that they were well assured, as they of the primitive church might very well be, of its being the only instituted and legitimate one?"‡

Venema.—"It is without controversy, that baptism, in the primitive church, was administered by immersion into water, and not by sprinkling. The essential act of baptizing, in the second century, consisted, not in sprinkling, but in immersion into water, in the name of each person in the Trinity. Concerning immersion, the words

* Def. of Hist. of Inf. Bap., pp. 131, 140.
† Orgines Eccles. B. xi. c. xi.
‡ Of the Sacram. of Bap. Part iii. p. 58.

and phrases that are used, sufficiently testify; and that it was performed in a river, a pool, or a fountain. To the essential rite of baptism, in the third century, pertained immersion, and not aspersion, except in cases of necessity, and it was accounted a half-perfect baptism. Immersion, in the fourth century, was one of those acts that were considered as essential to baptism;—nevertheless, aspersion was used in the last moments of life, on such as were called clinics—and also, where there was not a sufficient quantity of water."*

Salmasius.—" The ancients did not baptize, otherwise than by immersion, either once or thrice; except clinics, or persons confined to their beds, who were baptized in a manner of which they were capable; not in the entire laver as those who plunge the head under water, but the whole body had water poured upon it. (Cypr. iv. Epist. vii.) Thus Novatian when sick, received baptism, being sprinkled, not baptized." Euseb. vi. Hist. C. xliii.†

J. H. Fritsch, Bib. Theology, of 1820, vol. iii. p. 507. —" With infant baptism, still another change in the outward form of baptism was introduced, that of sprinkling with water, instead of the former practice of immersion."

In some of the above quotations my readers will notice a reference to "trine immersions," the candidate being immersed three times. This, however, was confessed to be an addition to the original act enjoined by

---

* Hist. Eccles. Secul. i. § 138; Secul. ii. § 100; Secul. iii. § 51; Secul. iv. § 110.

† Apud Witsu Æcon. Fæd. L. iv. c. xvi. § 13.

Christ. Tertullian declares that it was "doing somewhat more than the Gospel required." Basil* and Jerome† place it among those rites of the Church, derived from apostolic tradition.

Trine immersion continued to be practised in the West, as well as the East, till the end of the sixth century, when it was decreed by the fourth council of Toledo, that the primitive baptism by a single immersion should be restored.

In the third century we begin to find a substitute for immersion allowed in extreme cases. It being held impossible for any one to be saved without baptism, and this being impracticable with extremely ill and dying people, water was poured around them, as well as on them. Mark, however, this was not regarded as baptism, but only as a substitute in cases of necessity. The Greek word to express this act was not *Baptizo*, but *perikeo* (to pour around.) The first case we read of is that of Novatian, in the third century. Here is Eusebius's account of it. "Who, assisted by the exorcists, (having fallen into a dangerous disease, and being supposed near to death,) he received (the rite,) being poured round (*perikutheis*) on the bed on which he lay; if indeed, it is proper to say that such a one could receive (the rite.")

The following is a translation of the note of Valesius, on the word *perikutheis*.—" Rufinus rightly translates this *perfusum* (poured about.) For those who were

---

* Basil de Sd. Sanct. cap. xxvii. † Hieron. cont. Lucif. c. iv.

sick, were baptized in bed, since they could not be immersed by the priest, they were only poured (*perfundibantur*) with water. Therefore, baptism of this kind was not customary, and was esteemed imperfect as being what appeared to be received by men laboring under delirium, not willingly, but from fear of death. In addition, since baptism properly signifies immersion, a pouring of this sort could hardly be called baptism. Wherefore, clinics (for thus were they called who had received baptism of this sort) were forbidden to be promoted to the rank of the presbytery, by the twelfth canon of the council of Neo-Cæsarea."

Baronius says:—"Those who were baptized upon their beds were not called Christians but clinics."*

Cyprian (in reply to Magnus, third century.)—"You ask, dear son, what I think of those, who, in sickness, receive the sacred ordinance; whether, since they are not washed (*loti*) in the saving water, but have it poured on them, (*perfusi*,) they are to be esteemed right Christians. In the saving sacraments, when necessity obliges, and God grants his indulgence, *abridgements* of divine things (*divina compendia*) will confer the whole on believers."†

Monks of Cressy, A. D. 754.—"Is it lawful, in case of necessity occasioned by sickness, to baptize an infant by pouring water on its head, from a cup, or the hands!"‡

---

* Annales Eccl. Cæsaris Baronii, &c. Moguntiæ. 1523, An. 254, sect. ix. p. 208.

† Epistola ad Magnum, Edit. Paris, 1643.

‡ Apud Labbei Concilia, Tom. vi. p. 1650.

Pope Stephen III. (in reply to the Monks of Cressy.)—
"Such a baptism, performed in such a case of necessity, shall be accounted valid."*

Basnage.—"This (the response of Stephen, in the year 754) is accounted the first law against immersion. The Pontiff, however, did not dispense with immersion, except in case of extreme necessity. This law, therefore, did not change the mode of dipping, in public baptisms; and it was not until five hundred and fifty-seven years after, that the legislature in a council at Ravenna, in the year 1311, declared immersion and pouring indifferent."†

The subjoined quotations from the profoundest Pædobaptist ecclesiastical writers settle this matter, showing that in the age directly succeeding the times of the apostles, and many ages afterwards, immersion was the only baptism,—a substitute was never thought of except in cases of extreme illness, and this substitute was never defended as apostolical, but only as a thing of necessity.

Neander, vol. i. p. 361.—"Only with the sick was there an exception," in regard to immersion.

Winer, in his lectures on Archæology, in manuscript.—
"Affusion was at first applied only to the sick, but was gradually introduced for others after the seventh century, and in the thirteenth became the prevailing practice in

---

* Apud Labbei Concilia, Tom. vi. p. 1650.

† Monumenta, vol. i. Præfat c. v. § 4, in Robinson's Hist. of Bap. c. xxxiii.

the West. But the Eastern Church had retained immersion alone as valid.

Von Cöln, in his new edition of Munscher.—"Only with the sick was baptism administered by aspersion."

Stroth's Eusebius, vol. i. p. 506.—"Baptism was administered to those on beds of sickness by sprinkling and pouring; in other cases it was at that time by immersion."

Geiseler's Ch. Hist., Ger. Ed., vol. ii. p. 274.—"For the sake of the sick, the rite of sprinkling was introduced."

Du Fresne's Lat. Glossary, on the word *Clinici.*—"From the custom of baptizing by pouring or sprinkling the sick, who could not be immersed (which is properly baptism,) was introduced the custom which now prevails in the Western Church."

CHAPTER XI.

I HAVE now finished this part of my subject, and I put it to the conscience of my reader, whether there be a shadow of a doubt as to what is baptism. If a jury of impartial men were empanneled to decide this cause, would they leave their seats? If a wife loves her husband, would she require half this evidence to ascertain what is his will? If a voice from heaven should proclaim, that all who are not baptized before to-morrow night shall be destroyed, would you rest satisfied with having been sprinkled or poured upon?

Do not talk to me about the quantity of water,—Christ commands you to be immersed, have you obeyed him? You now perceive that the question is not about the form, but the thing itself. I care not in what mode you are immersed, so that you are immersed; but without immersion there can be no baptism.

And do not say, we lay too much stress on baptism. Is this so? Or is it not that our brethren lay too little stress on it? Upon this point I adjure you not to upbraid us, but to obey Christ. The question about what is essential to salvation, is unworthy of a Christian, for it betrays a disposition to disobey every precept where there is a prospect of impunity. I will not, therefore, touch that question. This examining with accuracy how far a man may go on the verge of hell, is to me a terrible calculation. This trying how close one can graze the edge of damnation, is an experiment which alarms, frightens, appals me. I will have nothing to do with a speculation so perilous—a casuistry belonging, not to the religion of love, which bides and yearns for the test, but to a mercenary religion, the religion of a selfish soul. I will have nothing to do with this conspiracy against the sovereignty of Jesus Christ; but I leave with you two subjects, and I beg you to ponder them seriously.

First, listen to the language of pious men of different ages.

Barnabus.—"We go down into the water full of sins and pollutions, but come up again, bringing forth fruit having in our hearts the fear and hope which are in Jesus by the Spirit."

H. Wall.—"There is not any one Christian writer, of any antiquity in any language, but who understands it (John, iii. 5, 'Except a man be born of water and the Spirit he cannot enter into the kingdom of God,') of baptism; and if it be not so understood, it is difficult to give an account how a person is born of water, any more than born of wood."*

Justin Martyr.—"Then we bring them to some place where there is water, and they are regenerated by the same way of regeneration by which we were regenerated; for they are washed in water (*en to udati*) in the name of God, the Father and Lord of all things, and of our Saviour Jesus Christ, and of the Holy Spirit; for Christ says, Unless you be regenerated you cannot enter into the kingdom of heaven."

Tertullian.—"Let them be made Christians when they can know Christ. What need their guiltless age make such haste to the forgiveness of sins."

Origen.—"The baptism of the church is given for the forgiveness of sins."

Calvin.—"Baptism resembles a legal instrument properly attested, by which he assures us that all our sins are cancelled, effaced and obliterated, so that they will never appear in his sight, or come into his remembrance, or be imputed to us. For he commands all who believe

* 4th London edition, p. 116, vol. 1. A. D. 1829.

to be baptized for the remission of their sins. Therefore those who have imagined that baptism is nothing more than a mark or sign by which we profess our religion before men, as soldiers wear the insignia of their sovereign as a mark of their profession, have not considered that which was the principal thing in baptism; which is that we ought to receive it with this promise, 'He that believeth and is baptized shall be saved.'"*

John Wesley, in his comment on the New Testament, p. 350,—"Baptism administered to real penitents, is both a means and a seal of pardon. Nor did God ordinarily in the primitive church bestow this (pardon) on any, unless through this means."

Barnes (on Mark, xvi. 16.)—"It is worthy of remark that Jesus has made baptism of so much importance. He did not say, indeed, that a man could not be saved without baptism, but he has strongly implied that where this is neglected, knowing it to be a command of the Saviour, it endangers the salvation of the soul. Faith and baptism are the beginnings of a Christian life; the one the beginning of piety in the soul, the other of its manifestation before men, or of a profession of religion. And no man can tell how much he endangers his eternal interest by being ashamed of Christ before men."

My readers will not understand me as concurring in all these quotations. I regard baptism just as I do any other command, and I dare not trench upon God's prerogative, and decide what is to be the consequence in

* Inst. i. 4. cxv. p. 327.

eternity of disobedience to any command. To the following declarations, however, we are all bound to submit, and my second subject for your reflection is, these passages. Construe them as you will, can you believe the Bible, and yet trifle with baptism? The language is that of God himself, and I implore my reader not to pass it lightly, but to take solemn heed to words, one jot or tittle of which shall not pass away, when the heavens and the earth have passed away. "He that believeth and is baptized shall be saved." "The like figure whereunto baptism doth now also save us, not the putting away the filth of the flesh, but the answer of a good conscience toward God by the resurrection of Jesus Christ." "Now when they heard this they were pricked to their heart, and said unto Peter and to the rest of the apostles, Men and brethren, what shall we do? Then Peter said unto them, Repent and be baptized, every one of you, in the name of Jesus Christ, for the remission of sins." "Arise and be baptized, and wash away thy sins."

My dear reader, these are the words of God himself, and have a care how you slight them. This matter is of much more concern to you than it can be to me; let me then beseech you not to regard it as a point of controversial theology, but of deep practical interest. One-half the world never comprehended, and the other half have long since become thoroughly sick of those metaphysical abstractions which have almost supplanted the gospel of Christ. The matter before you, however, is not an abstraction; it is a plain duty which meets you at the very threshold of the Christian course, and which you may not evade without insult to the Saviour and peril to your soul.

For myself, I wish only to lead you to the truth. When the prophet commanded Naaman to go and wash in the Jordan, he "turned away in a rage." "Then his servants came near and spake unto him and said, 'My father, if the prophet had bid thee do some great thing, wouldst thou not have done it? How much rather, then, when he saith to thee, Wash and be clean.'" The humble but faithful office of such a servant is all I covet. God forbid that I should ascribe salvation to any thing except the blood of Christ. On every page of the Bible I behold nothing but the cross, and its amazing retinue of suffering and glory. For me, patriarch and prophet and apostle all utter one voice, all point to Calvary, and cry, Behold the Lamb of God, which taketh away the sin of the world! As a minister, as a sinner, I have no theme, no hope, but Christ Jesus and him crucified. On him and him alone, on the redundant merit of his atonement, my soul leans with a recumbency, a confidence, a delight unspeakble and full of glory.

But suffer me to come near to you and warn you that the gospel is to be "*obeyed*,"* as well as "*believed*." If Jesus had required of you the bitterest sacrifice, would

---

* "Being made perfect, he became the author of eternal salvation unto all them that *obey* him." "The Lord Jesus shall be revealed from heaven with his mighty angels, in flaming fire, taking vengeance on them that know not God, and that *obey not*

you not make it? Can any thing be worthy of the name of sacrifice when compared with salvation? How much rather then, with what joy, should you obey him, when he offers you so great a salvation, and says, "He that beliveth and is baptized shall be saved."

the gospel of our Lord Jesus Christ." "Blessed are they that *do* his commandments, that they may have right to the tree of life, and may enter in through the gates into the city." Heb. v. 9. 2 Thess. i. 7, 8. Rev. xxii. 14.

PART SECOND.
INFANT BAPTISM

In using the above caption to this part of my subject, I suppose that there has been a baptism, viz: an immersion. I make this supposition to relieve me from the pain of employing any phrase which can wound any body. I have read and heard, with unspeakable sorrow, the language sometimes applied by Baptists to infant baptism. However unscriptural, the practice is yet regarded by many as sacred, and I am incapable of any want of respect for their feelings.

I suppose, then, that there has been an immersion of the child, and this question now arises, is the baptism of an infant, Christian Baptism? In other words, Christ has commanded his disciples to be baptized; is a parental act, a mere *opus operatum*, performed upon an unconscious child, the act which Christ requires, so that the child can be said to have obeyed the command of Christ? This is the question, and to state such a question is to answer it.

In entering upon this topic, let it be observed that there is no difference between us and our Pædobaptist brethren, as to the duty of parents to *dedicate* their children to God. From the entire Scriptures, and especially from those passages where "they brought children to Christ, and he said, 'Forbid them not,' and put his hands on them, and blessed them," we have abundant warrants for taking our offspring in the arms of faith, and presenting them to the Redeemer, and imploring his benediction on them. Dedicate your children to God. Supplicate for them Christ's blessing, without which nothing is blessed. But do not, in the very act of seeking his favor, suffer that to be done which cannot be pleasing in his sight, if it be unscriptural.

Another remark. Our Pædobaptist brethren and ourselves have no controversy about the *salvation* of infants. If any man believes that infants, with or without water, will be damned, I have nothing to say to that man. One of the calumnies clandestinely circulated against the Baptists is, that they hold this horrible doctrine. We are the last denomination which ought to be suspected of it. Indeed, one reason why every Christian ought to set his face against infant baptism is, that it originated in this blasphemous heresy, and still squints at it. Our opponents dare not openly avow, and most of them abhor, a tenet so abominable; but by indirections and hints about "covenant mercies," some of them are still too often found working upon the feelings of parents, and carrying their point by exciting I know not what vague fears and hopes as to some possible influence of baptism on the child's eternal destiny. While ministers do such things, no wonder this error is perpetuated. But it is surely wrong thus to tamper with the dearest feelings of the human heart. It is a wickedness to appeal to the passions, when the only appeal should be to the word of God. I am, myself, a parent. For worlds would I not withhold from my children any means of securing for them God's blessing. I covet this for my children far above all the wealth and honors of earth. But worlds could not tempt me to an act in which my child is concerned, unless I had God's clear warrant for it. Nor for worlds would I profane the tender affections implanted in a parent's bosom, by enlisting them in behalf of error and disobedience.

As baptism is a positive command, and as the Commission is the only authority for baptizing, it is manifest that our opponents must show that infants are comprehended in this Commission. The burden of proof rests upon them. I waive, however, this clear logical right, and undertake to prove the negative. In doing so I ask the candid attention of my reader. Duty to Christ, ourselves, and our children, demands of us all a calm, and thorough, and patient investigation of this subject.

CHAPTER I.

In this chapter I ask my reader's attention to the Commission. As if to preclude the possibility of any misapprehension, the Holy Spirit has published this Commission twice, and in different phraseology. In Matthew it is, " Go ye therefore, and teach all nations, baptizing them in the name of the Father, and of the Son, and of the Holy Ghost; teaching them to observe all things whatsoever I have commanded you : and lo, I am with you always, even unto the end of the world." In Mark it is "Go ye into all the world, and preach the gospel to every creature. He that believeth and is baptized, shall be saved: but he that beliveth not, shall be damned." Now I ask were ever instructions given with more plainness and precision?

First, the persons are first to be "*taught.*" "Go teach all nations." This is to precede baptism. And as this is the only Commission by which any one can be baptized, it settles the whole question, and forever excludes infants. It is idle to say that this is the law of baptism for grown persons. It is the whole law. If infants are to be baptized, there must be another Commission. Let that be produced, and I will obey it. But with this Commission before me, it is as plain as the sun in the firmament that, before baptizing any one, I am to teach him; and, therefore, that infants are not to be baptized.

The only answer which has been attempted to this demonstration is, that the Commission means, "Go make disciples by baptizing." Here again our brethren object to their own translation; but all objections are futile. A moment's examination dissipates this pretext.

In the first place, are our opponents really prepared to adopt this version, and say that Christ requires his ministers to make disciples by baptizing only? "Go, make all nations disciples by baptizing them." Is this the gospel? Does baptizing a man make him a disciple of Christ? and is it the duty of ministers and missionaries to baptize every body the first thing? If the language of the Commission be as our opponents would make it, then this must be done.

In the next place, if this monstrous construction be put upon the Commission, and disciples are to be manufactured by water alone, yet infants would still be excluded. However disciples are made, it is absurd to call an unconscious infant a "disciple." What is a disciple? He is, says Webster, "a learner," "one who receives instruction from another, as the disciples of Plato," "a follower." Can an infant be a disciple of Christ? Jesus himself tells us what it is to be his disciple: "If any one will be my disciple, let him deny himself, and take up his cross and follow me." How preposterous to say that an infant is Christ's disciple, and that disciples are made by water.

But the Commission cannot be thus perverted. It is express. The word rendered "*teach*" is *Matheteusate*, and means "*teach.*" Bloomfield translates it, "*Convert them to the faith.*" The word has a precise, definite meaning, and always imports giving instruction. It occurs frequently in the New Testament, and invariably has this signification. The same writer, Matthew, uses it in ch. xiii. 52, "A scribe instructed (*Matheteutheis*) unto the kingdom," &c. It occurs again in Acts, xiv. 21, "And when they had preached the gospel to that city, and had taught (*Matheteusantes*) many," &c. The advocates of infant baptism would mutilate the Commission, striking out of it this word, this previous teaching, and making the first act required to be baptism. Christ commanded us to teach, then baptize, then teach. They expunge the first command, and say, "Go baptize and then teach."

As if to shut and bar out everything like a cavil, Mark

tells us what the teaching is. He says, "*Preach the gospel* to every creature;" the Holy Spirit thus declaring that the "*teaching*" enjoined is the "*preaching of the gospel.*" Matthew says, "Go *teach* all nations, baptizing them," i. e. baptizing them after teaching them. Mark says: "*Preach the gospel* to every creature; he that believeth and is baptized shall be saved." The Commission, therefore, plainly requires, 1st, Teaching or preaching the gospel; 2d, Faith; 3d, Baptism.

In short, observe what is to follow baptism. The persons baptized are to be taught to observe all of Christ's commandments; "teaching them to observe all things whatsoever I have commanded you." How irresistible the conclusion, that the baptized persons are supposed to be capable, first, of being taught the principles of the gospel before baptism, and directly after, of entering upon a life of actual obedience.

The argument from the Commission is so simple that every unprejudiced mind must yield to it. Vainly has this document been stretched on a Procrustean bed, and in derision of Scripture, amid the outcries of truth, and grammar, and common sense, been violently mangled; its testimony is distinct, conclusive, irrevocable. Even if infant baptism could be established by other portions of the Bible, it would not, could not, be baptism under the Commission. The apostle says there is but "one baptism;" if infant baptism be scriptural there are two baptisms, one under the Commission, and one entirely distinct from this. Nor would this latter act be any substitute for the former. When old enough, it would still be the duty of the child to believe, and be baptized in obedience to the Commission.

Grotius.—"Seeing there are two kinds of teaching, one by way of introduction to the first principles, the other by way of more perfect instruction; the former seems to be intended by the word *matheteuein*, for that is, as it were, to initiate into discipline, and is to go before baptism; the latter is intended by the word *didaskein*, which is here placed after baptism." In loc.

Calvin.—"Because Christ requires teaching before baptizing, and will have believers only admitted to baptism, baptism does not seem to be rightly administered, except faith precede. Under this pretence, the Anabaptists have loudly clamored against Pœdobaptism." In Harm. Evang. Comment. ad. loc.

Dr. Barrow.—"What the action itself enjoined is, what the manner and form thereof, is apparent by the words of our Lord's institution: Going forth, saith he, teach, or disciple, all nations, baptizing them. The action is baptizing or immersing in water; the object thereof, those persons, of any nation, whom his ministers can by their instruction and persuasion render disciples; that is, such as do sincerely believe the truth of his doctrine, and seriously resolve to obey his commandments." Works, vol. i. p. 518, edit. 1722.

Saurin.—"In the primitive church, instruction preceded baptism, agreeably to the order of Jesus Christ: 'Go, teach all nations, baptizing them.' Thus, likewise, we understand St. Peter, when he says that the baptism which saves us, is 'not the putting away of the filth of the flesh, but the answer of a good conscience.' The answer of a good conscience, is that account which the Catechumen gives of his faith and knowledge. Whence it came to pass, that the ancients usually called a baptized person one that was illuminated." Serm. tom. 1, pp. 301, 302. Le Haye, edit. 3d.

Vossius.—" Respecting adults, it is required that they be taught the Christian religion and profess it, before they be baptized; for this the very institution of baptism teaches. (Matt. xxviii. 19; Mark, xvi. 15, 16.) We are taught the same thing by the practice of John the Baptist, and of the apostles (Matt. iii. 1, 2; Luke, iii. 3; Acts, ii. 38, 41.") Disput. de Bap. disput. xii. § 3.

Dr. Doddridge.—"I render the word *Matheteusate*, proselyte, that it may be duly distinguished from *didaskontes*, teaching, (in the next verse,) with which our version confounds it. The former seems to import instruction in the essentials of religion, which it was necessary adult persons should know and submit to, before they could regularly be admitted to baptism; the latter may relate to those more particular admonitions in regard to Christian faith and practice, which were to be built on that foundation." Note on the place.

Limborch.—"They could not make disciples, unless by teaching. By that instruction, disciples were brought to the faith before they were baptized." (Mark, xvi. 15, 16.) Instit. l. v. c. lxvii. § 7.

Dr. Whitby.—"*Matheteuein* here, is 'to preach the gospel to all nations.' and to engage them to believe it, in order to their profession of that faith by baptism; as seems apparent (1) from the parallel Commission, Mark, xvi. 15, 'Go preach the gospel to every creature: he that believeth and is baptized shall be saved.' (2) From the Scripture notion of a disciple, that being still the same as a believer. If here it should be said that I yield too much to the Anti-Pædobaptists by saying, that to be made disciples here is to be taught to believe in Christ, I desire any one to tell me how the apostles could *matheteuein*, make a disciple of a heathen or an unbelieving Jew, without being *mathetai*, or teachers of them; whether they were not sent to preach to those that could hear, and to teach them to whom they preached, that 'Jesus was the Christ,' and only to baptize them when they did believe this." Annotat. on the place.

Venema. — " 'Go,' says our Lord to the apostles, 'teach all nations, baptizing them in the name of the Father, and of the Son, and of the Holy Ghost; teaching them to observe all things whatsoever I have commanded you.' This is an excellent passage, and explains the whole nature of baptism. Before persons were baptized, it was necessary for them to believe the preaching of the apostles, which faith they were to profess in baptism. For the word *Matheteuein*, in the style of the New Testament, does not signify barely to admit into a school and instruction, but to admit after the doctrine is believed, and after a previous subjection to the school." Dissertat. Sac. i. 2, c. xiv. § 6.

Mr. Baxter.—" Go disciple me all nations, baptizing them. As for those that say they are discipled by baptizing, and not before baptizing, they speak not the sense of that text, nor that which is true or rational, if they mean it absolutely as so spoken; else why should one be baptized more than another? This is not like some occasional historical mention of baptism, but it is the very Commission of Christ to his apostles for preaching and baptizing, and purposely expresseth their several works, in their several places and order. Their first task is by teaching to make *disciples*, who are by Mark called '*believers*.' The second work is to baptize them, whereunto is annexed the promise of their salvation. The third work is to teach them all other things, which are afterwards to be learned in the school of Christ. To contemn this order is to renounce all rules of order; for where can we expect to find it if not here? I profess my conscience is fully satisfied from this text that it is one sort of faith, even saving, that must go before baptism, and the profession whereof the minister must expect." Disputat. of Right to Sac. pp. 91, 149, 150.

When Christ gives a command, and the command is plain, our duty is to obey. All objections are impious, for they impeach the Divine wisdom and goodness. With reference to the Commission, the cavils sometimes uttered scarcely deserve notice.

For instance, it is said, If infants cannot be baptized under the Commission, then infants cannot be saved; for the language is, "He that believeth and is baptized shall be saved." To which I reply, that infants are neither saved nor baptized under the Commission. Is it not in fact, a most glaring folly to suppose that the

Commission is for infants at all? We believe that infants are saved through the atonement of Jesus, but for them there was no necessity for any Commission. To talk about preaching the gospel to infants, is to use the language of insanity. Both infants and adults are saved by the blood of Christ. Of adults, Christ requires that they believe and be baptized, but he does not require either of infants. Indeed, it is absurd to speak of requiring any thing of infants. God may enjoin on parents a duty towards their children, as in the case of circumcision; the Commission, however, does not require a parental, but a personal obedience. It suspends the salvation of adults on certain specified terms; but faith is impossible in an infant, and, therefore, it does not require of him either faith or baptism which is to follow faith.

Again, we are told that "there is no command not to baptize infants;" but what sort of logic is this? The only authority to baptize any body is the Commission. The Commission specifies, as subjects for baptism, those who are taught and believe. Does not this shut out those who are not taught, and do not believe? Does not a command to circumcise males exclude females? A merchant commissions his agent to purchase an invoice of silk goods; what would he think if, besides the bales of silk, his agent should send him a supply of lumber, saying that, as he was not forbidden to purchase lumber, he regarded the order as including boards as well as silk? No child ever reasoned on other matters as Doctors of Divinity do about Christ's Commission, and yet never was there a document more unequivocal. A command to teach and baptize the taught, *is* a command not to baptize infants who are incapable of being taught. It is a waste of time to attempt argument with a man who does not perceive this. Surely Paul must have encountered people laboring under this incurable obliquity of mind, when he so importunately prayed to be "delivered from unreasonable men."

It is difficult to believe that the authors of one or two essays are serious when they cite, as bearing on this topic, the language of Paul, in 2 Thess. iii. 10. He says: "If any man would not work, neither let him eat." They exclaim, "According to your reasoning, as infants cannot work, therefore infants are not to eat." Are these writers in earnest? The only authority to baptize is the Commission. Is this verse the only authority for eating? Is God here publishing the commission under which people are permitted to eat? The apostle is exhorting to industry; he mentions certain busy bodies, who would not "work at all;" and says that those who would not work ought not to be supported, but be left to feel the wholesome discipline of want. Was there in Thessalonica an idiot who could infer from this direction, that infants were to be left to starve? The command to work has reference to those who can work.; and so the command to believe and be baptized has reference to those who can believe, and not to those who cannot.

That under the Commission there must be faith before baptism, is a truth so manifest, that, when infant baptism was introduced, there was always some device to meet the difficulty. Indeed, at first there was no difference between the baptismal formulary used for infants, and that used for adults. In each case there was required a confession of faith; but as the infants could not speak, there was introduced a third party, unknown to the Scriptures, and whose very existence confesses an innovation on the baptism of the Bible. This third party was sponsors, and through these sponsors the child was really supposed to speak.

That faith and repentance must be personal acts, and that no one can believe or repent by proxy, is a self-evident proposition. The fathers, therefore, who first baptized children, conferred the rite, not on account of the faith of the sponsor or parent, (this is comparatively a modern "invention," which men have "sought out,") but on account of the *faith of the child itself*. They could neither baptize a subject who had not faith, nor swallow the absurdity of vicarious faith. They, therefore, affirmed that the child had faith, and took the answers of the sponsors as the real language of the child. In the Greek and Roman Catholic Churches, this monstrous fiction is still preserved; and the Episcopal Church follows them. Here are the baptismal services of the Greek and Episcopal Churches, in which my readers will see that faith is required before baptism, and the infant is really supposed to believe.

FORM OF THE GREEK CHURCH.

QUESTIONS BEFORE BAPTISM.

The priest then turns the catechumen to the West, and saith: "*Doth thou renounce the devil and all his works, all his angels, and all his service, and his pomps?*"

The catechumen then answereth, or his sponsor, if it be a pagan, or a child, and saith: "*I do renounce.*"

(Question asked and answered three times.)

Priest. *Hast thou then renounced the devil?*

Catechumen. *I have renounced.*

Priest. "*Blow and spit upon him,*"—*which he does; and the priest then turns him to the East, holding his hands down, and saith to him:* "*Art thou joined to Christ?*"

Catech. *I am joined.*

Priest. *Hast thou been joined unto Christ?*

Catech. *I have been joined.*

Priest. *Dost thou believe in him?*

Catech. *I believe in him as the living God:* (*and then repeats the creed.*)

Priest. *Hast thou been joined unto Christ?*

Catech. *I have been joined.*

Priest. *Worship him.*

Catech. (*Bowing.*) *I worship the Father, &c.*

Concludes with the blessing and prayer.

FORM OF THE EPISCOPAL CHURCH.

"*Minister.* Dost thou, in the name of this child, renounce the devil and all his works the vain pomps and glory of the world, with all covetous desires of the same, and the sinful desires of the flesh; so that thou wilt not follow, nor be led by them?

"*Answer.* I renounce them all; and by God's help, will endeavor not to follow, nor be led by them." (THIS IS "IN THE NAME OF THE CHILD.")

"*Minister.* Dost thou believe all the articles of the Christian Faith, as contained in the Apostles'. creed?

"*Answer.* I do. (*Is this* "*in the name of the child*" *too?*—i. e. "*in the name of this child I do believe?*"

"*Minister.* Wilt thou be baptized in this faith?

"*Answer.* That is my desire. (*Here we have the child.*)

"*Minister.* Will thou then obediently keep God's holy will and commandments, and walk in the same all the days of thy life?

"*Answer.* I will by God's help." (*This is the child.*)

Lest any should doubt the possibility of people's really teaching that the infant believes, I quote the following passage from the highest Pædobaptist authority. It is from Bingham's Antiquities of the Christian Church, vol. iii. p. 241.—"Two things, indeed, were anciently required of sponsors, as their proper duty. (1.) To answer in their names (that is, *of the infants*) to all the interrogatories of baptism. If any one thinks these promises related only to what the sponsors promised for themselves, and not in the name of the child, he may be informed more clearly from others (than Tertullian.)

Gennadius tells us these promises for infants, and such as were incapable of learning, were made after the usual manner of interrogatories in baptism. St. Augustine,* more particularly acquaints us with the form then used, which was 'Doth this child believe in God? Doth he turn to God?' which is the same as renouncing the devil, and making a covenant with Christ. And he professes he would not admit any child to baptism, whose sponsor he had reason to believe did not make these promises and responses sincerely for him. Of the form and practice, then, there is no doubt; only it seemed a great difficulty to Bishop Boniface, and, as such, he proposed it to St. Augustine, 'How it could be said, with truth, that a child believed, or renounced the devil, or turned to God, who had no thought or apprehension of those things? .... Since no one, therefore, would promise either for his future morals or his present thoughts, how is it that when parents, or sponsors, present their children in baptism, they answer and say, the children do those things which that age does not so much as think of?' To this Augustine answers, 'That the child is only said to believe, because he receives the sacrament of faith and conversion, which entitles him to the name of a believer; for the sacraments, because of the resemblance between them, and the things represented by them, do carry the name of the things represented. . . . And upon this account, when it is answered that an infant believes, who has not yet any knowledge or habit of faith, the meaning of the answer is, that he has faith be-

* Aug. Epist xxiii. ad Bonifac.

cause of the sacrament of faith, and is converted to God because of the sacrament of conversion; for these answers appertain to the celebration of the sacraments?'" Was the like ever heard out of Bedlam?

Those who introduced infant baptism acted consistently, and admitted infants to the Lord's Supper also, and with reason; for as the child really had faith, and was baptized on its own faith, it had a right to the Supper. So indisputable is the antiquity of infant communion, that Lord King, in his celebrated work on the Church, (p. 196,) founds upon this practice an argument for the antiquity of infant baptism. He says: "That infants were baptized, will be evident from this single consideration: baptism was always precedent to the Lord's Supper; and none were admitted to receive the eucharist till they were baptized." This is so obvious to every man that it needs no proof; if any one doubts it, he may find it clearly asserted in the Second Apology of Justin Martyr, p. 97. Children received the eucharist in the primitive Church, which is also a thing so well known, as that for the proof of it, I shall only urge one passage of Cyprian's, where he tells a long story of a sucking girl, who so violently refused to taste the sacramental wine, "that the deacon was obliged forcibly to open her lips, and to pour down the consecrated wine."*

I add the following authorities as to infant communion.

* Diaconus reluctanti licet de sacramento calicis infudit. De Lapais, § xx. p. 284.

Apostolical Constitutions.—"First let the bishop receive, then the presbyters, &c.; among the women, the deaconesses, virgins and widows; after that, the children, and then all the people in order."*

Augustine.—" 'Except ye eat the flesh of the Son of Man, and drink his blood, ye have no life in you.' And dare any one be so bold as to say, that this sentence does not appertain to little children, or that they can have life without partaking of this body and this blood?"†

In Gregory's Sacramentarum,‡ there is an order, "that infants should be allowed to suck the breast before the holy communion, if necessity so required." The old *Ordo Romanus* of the ninth century directs, "That infants, after they are baptized, should not eat any food, nor suck the breast, without great necessity, till they had communicated in the sacrament of the body of Christ."

Salmasius.—"It was the invariable practice to give the eucharist immediately after they were baptized. Afterwards the opinion prevailed, that no one could be saved unless he were baptized, so the custom of baptizing infants was introduced. And because to adult catechumens, as soon as they were baptized, no space of time intervening, the eucharist was given, so after Pædobaptism was introduced, this was also done in the case of infants."§

---

* Const. lib. viii. cap. 12.

† Aug. de Peccator. Merit. lib. 1, cap. 20.

‡ Gregor. Sacr. in Office, Sabbat. Sanct.

§ Salmasius, (a learned Roman Catholic writer,) in libro de Transubstantione contra H. Grotium, p. 495.

Bossuet.—"The church has always believed, and still believes, that infants are capable of receiving the eucharist, as well as baptism, and finds no more obstacle to their communion in the words of St. Paul, 'Let a man examine himself, and so let him eat,' than she finds to their baptism in these words of our Lord, 'Teach and baptize.' But as she knew the eucharist could not be absolutely necessary to their salvation, after they had received the full remission of sins in baptism, she believed it was a matter of discipline to give or not give the communion in this age; thus it is that during the first eleven or twelve centuries she, for good reasons, gave it; and for other reasons, equally good, has since then ceased to give it."*

When we come to the period of the Reformation we find, in the history of infant baptism, one of the most melancholy evidences of the tenacity with which good men and great men will cling to old hereditary sanctities. Instead of restoring Christian baptism, and thus extricating themselves from this, as from other corruptions, Luther and Calvin both allowed infant baptism to remain, and practiced it. But how did they solve the difficulty presented in the Commission? Did they adopt so preposterous a system as that which confers baptism before there is faith? They did not. To them, as to Baptists, the command of Christ was perfectly plain. He requires, first, faith, then baptism. Luther and Calvin, therefore, maintained, though most strangely, and in

* Bossuet Traite de Communion sous les deux Especes, part 1, page 3.

direct contradiction to their great doctrines of justification by faith and the necessity of the New Birth, that, somehow or other, children really had faith.

Here is Luther's solution of the matter. Let common sense say whether, if infant baptism were in the Bible, such a mind as that of the Great Reformer could have been driven to such a shift, in order to make out an apology for it. "Therefore we here say and conclude, that the children believe in baptism itself, and have their own faith, which God works in them through the intercession and hearty offering of the sponsors, in the faith of the Christian Church; and that is what we call the power of another's faith; not that any one can be saved through that, but that he hereby (that is, through another's intercession and aid) may obtain a faith of his own from God, by which he is saved. Their own faith, in which they are baptized and believe for themselves."*

As for Calvin, although he insisted on the perseverance of saints, and the doctrines of depravity and election and reprobation, yet, when he has to defend infant baptism, he contradicts all these articles, and with singular inconsistency maintains that infants are, by natural birth, the heirs of God. He says, "To remove all doubt, this principle must always be maintained—that baptism is not conferred upon infants, in order that they may become the children and heirs of God, but because they are already in that rank and position with God, the grace of adoption is sealed in their flesh by baptism;

* Works of Martin Luther, edited by Walch. Wittenberg, vol. xi. pp. 667, 672.

otherwise Anabaptists would be right in excluding them from baptism. Alioqui recte eos a baptismo arcerent Anabaptistæ."*

When we examine the modern creeds, we find on every side infinite confusion. That infants really have faith, is an absurdity which can now be no longer ventured; it is, therefore, generally abandoned. But how to defend their baptism without faith, perplexes our opponents, and divides them into conflicting and utterly irreconcilable factions.

Dr. Miller says: "After all, the whole weight of the objection, in this case, is founded on an entire forgetfulness of the main principle of the Pædobaptist system. It is forgotten that in every case of infant baptism, faith is required, and if the parents be sincere, is actually exercised. But it is required of the parents, not of the children; so that, if the parent really present his child in faith, the spirit of the ordinance is entirely met and answered."

Dr. Kurtz says: " Allow that the children were baptized on the ground of their father's faith, and all the mystery and difficulty of the passage vanish at once."

The Episcopalian baptizes infants because they are not members of the church, and that they may be "regenerated and grafted into the body of Christ's church." The Lutheran and Presbyterian baptize infants for a reason the very reverse of this, viz: because they are by birth members of Christ's church, and " as members of

* Calvin's Institutes, 2d edition, Strasburgh, A. D. 1352. Quoted in Henry's Life of Calvin, Hamburgh, 1835, vol. i. p. 325.

his church they ought to be baptized." In the Methodist baptismal service, baptism is declared to be "not only a sign of profession and mark of difference, whereby Christians are distiguished from others that are not baptized, but it is also a sign of regeneration, or the new birth," that is, a sign of what does not exist—that is, a false sign. From the essays written by my brethren of different denominations, I find it impossible to gather what they make of this rite; many of them regarding baptism as only a sort of ceremony by which a child is dedicated. In fine, an eminent Independent minister, Dr. Williams, places the whole matter on new ground, and insists that, as infants are members of the church in heaven, they ought not to be excluded from the "church militant." Infants in the church *militant!* Suppose, during the Revolution, some general had said, If we succeed, infants will be in the victorious nation; therfore, there must be infant regiments enlisted to fight in the army. "If any general (says Carson) should talk of raising an army of infants to oppose an invading enemy, he would at once be deemed insane, and his sovereign would not one moment longer entrust him to command; no, not though he were the Duke of Wellington. But when Doctors of Divinity speak like madmen, it is only the depth of their theological learning, and they are only the more admired."

CHAPTER II.

The argument from the Commission is so irrefragable, that I am willing to rest the whole question upon it. If, however, any one is still unconvinced, then I submit to his candor another argument, which ought to end this controversy. I mean the distinct intimations furnished by the instances of baptism recorded in the New Testament.

The first baptisms of which we have any account are those of John the Baptist. I subjoin all that the Bible tells respecting these. Matt. iii. 1.—"In those days came John the Baptist, preaching in the wilderness of Judea." Luke, iii. 3.—"And he came into all the country about Jordan, preaching the baptism of repentance for the remission of sins." Matt. iii. 2.—"And saying, repent ye, for the kingdom of heaven is at hand."

Acts, xiii. 24.—"John preached the baptism of repentance to all the people of Israel." Acts, xix. 4.—" Saying unto the people that they should believe on Him which should come after him, that is, on Christ Jesus."

Matt. iii. 5.—"Then went out to him Jerusalem and all Judea, and all the region round about Jordan, and were baptized of him in Jordan, confessing their sins." Mark, i. 4, 5.—" John did baptize in the wilderness, and preach the baptism of repentance for the remission of sins. And there went out to him all the land of Judea, and they of Jerusalem, and were all baptized of him in the river of Jordan, confessing their sins."

Matt. iii. 7, 8.—" But when he saw many of the Pharisees and Sadducees come to his baptism, he said unto them, O generation of vipers, who hath warned you to flee from the wrath to come? Bring forth, therefore, fruits meet for repentance. 9. And think not to say within yourselves, We have Abraham to our father; for I say unto you, that God is able of these stones to raise up children unto Abraham."

Now here it is evident that those who were baptized were none of them infants; for they "repented" and "confessed their sins." This is not all. John struck directly at the error of a hereditary claim to any privilege whatever in the church of Christ. Jesus tells us that the New Testament dispensation, or the gospel church system, was first introduced by John. "The law and the prophets were until John, since that time the kingdom of God is preached." John himself said, "Repent, for the kingdom of heaven (the gospel dispensation) is at hand." But now, in the very incipiency of the establishment of churches, observe what care to cut off every hope of any sort of right by descent. John not only confines his baptism to adults, but he utters this significant warning, "Think not to say within yourselves, We have Abraham to our father; for I say unto you, that God is able of these stones to raise up children unto Abraham."

From the baptism of John, we pass next to the baptism by the disciples while Jesus was with them, and here we find only adults as the subjects.

John, iv. 1, 2, 3.—" When, therefore, the Lord knew

how the Pharisees had heard that Jesus made and baptized more disciples than John, (though Jesus himself baptized not, but his disciples,) he left Judea, and departed again into Galilee."

From this passage we learn that Jesus (by his disciples) baptized none but "disciples whom he had made." If you wish to know whom he regarded as disciples, he tells you. He says, "Whosoever doth not bear his cross, and come after me, cannot be my disciple."

Having seen that no infants were baptized by John, or during the life of Christ, let us now take up, in order, the instances of baptism under the Commission. I have already shown that the Commission contemplates none but believers; we may rest assured then, that none else were baptized; and a glance at the cases will be enough to vindicate the apostles from the charge of having violated the plain instructions of their Master.

The first baptism under the Commission is that of Pentecost. Three thousand were then baptized; and yet it is certain there was not an infant among them, for it is said, "Then they that gladly received his word were baptized." (Acts, ii. 41.) What an overwhelming fact this. Compare this record with those of Pædobaptist churches. Was it ever known that three thousand were there baptized, and yet not a child among them? It is also said (v. 47,) "And the Lord added to the church daily such as should be saved." So, too, (ch. v. 14,) "And believers were the more added to the Lord, multitudes both of men and women."

The second baptism under the Commission is that of

Philip, at Samaria, (Acts, viii.) and here, again, we are told that the subjects were believers. "But when they believed Philip preaching the things concerning the kingdom of God, and the name of Jesus Christ, they were baptized, both men and women."

The third and fourth baptisms are those of the Eunuch, Acts, viii. and of Paul, Acts, ix. Believer's baptism in each case.

The fifth baptism is that of Cornelius and his friends, Acts, x. 42. There can be no question as to the subjects in this instance. Peter preaches to them, that "through his (Christ's) name, whosoever believeth in him shall receive remission of sins." (v. 43.) "While Peter yet spake these words, the Holy Ghost fell on all them which heard the word." (v. 44.) "Then answered Peter, can any man forbid water that these should not be baptized, which have received the Holy Ghost as well as we."

The sixth and seventh baptisms are those of Lydia, and the jailor, and their households. It is certain that Lydia and the jailor both believed before they were baptized. I shall presently advert to their households.

We come next to the persons baptized while Paul was at Corinth. It is said of these, "Many of the Corinthians, hearing, believed, and were baptized." (Acts, xviii. 8.) For some reason, it would appear that Paul himself baptized but few. Referring to this visit, he thus writes, (1 Cor. i. 14, 16,) "I thank God that I baptized none of you but Crispus and Gaius." "And I baptized also the household of Stephanas." I shall revert to this household again. It is plain from the account in Acts, that those baptized at Corinth "heard and believed." The last baptism mentioned in the Acts is that of certain disciples of Ephesus; but I need not dwell on this, as they were adult believers.

We have, thus, run over the history of baptism in the New Testament, and find that believers were the only subjects. Our opponents, however, reply that households were baptized, and that this furnishes a ground for administering the rite to infants; an argument this, which has been over and over exposed, and the fallacy of which ought surely to strike every thinking mind.

For, with the Commission before us, requiring faith as a prerequisite to baptism, and with the practice of the apostles, in strict conformity with that Commission, is it not strange to argue that, because in some instances, all the members of a family were baptized, therefore, there were infants in those families, and those infants were baptized? An officer is sent on the recruiting service, and his written orders are to "enlist able-bodied men." We find him faithful to his instructions in every case, and receiving none but able-bodied recruits. He tells us that, in a certain village, he "enlisted a father and all his sons;" would any body suspect him of having enlisted infants? Just as strange is the whole inference attempted from the mention of household baptisms. In the case supposed, the conclusion would be inevitable, that the father and his sons were all able-bodied men; and just so, it is certain that the members of families baptized under the Commission were believers.

What renders this inference from household baptisms still more glaringly false is, that the same inspired writer also speaks of "household faith." In Acts, xviii. 8, it is said, "And Crispus, the chief ruler of the synagogue, believed on the Lord with all his house." Were there infants among those believers? Yet to affirm this, would be just as rational as it is to pretend that there were infants, when it is said that "all in a house were baptized." Before this argument can be urged at all, our opponents must prove that there were infants in those families, and that they were baptized; neither of which can ever be shewn. The Commission, and the uniform practice under it, preclude such an idea.

The first household baptism I notice is that of Stephanas. In this family there were plainly no infants. They were baptized at Corinth, by Paul; and we are expressly informed that only believers were there baptized. "Many of the Corinthians hearing, believed and were baptized." (Acts, xviii. 8.) If farther testimony be needed, Paul himself supplies it. In 1 Cor. xvi. 15, he says: "Ye know the house of Stephanas, that it is the first fruit of Achaia; and they have *addicted themselves to the ministry of the saints.*"

Doddridge.—"They have set themselves, &c. This seems to imply that it was the generous care of the whole family to assist their fellow Christians; so that there was not a member of it which did not do its part." Fam. Expos.—Note on the place.

Guise.—"It, therefore, seems that the family of Stephanas were all adult believers, and so were baptized on their own personal profession of faith in Christ."—(In loc.)

Macknight.—"The family of Stephanas seems all to have been adults when they were baptized; for they are said, ch. xvi. 15, to have devoted themselves to the ministry of the saints." Apos. Epis.—Note on 1 Cor. i. 16.

The next household baptism is that of the jailor, Acts, xvi. 33, and here again there were plainly no infants. It is expressly said that Paul and Silas "Spake unto him the word of the Lord, and to *all that were in his house;*" and it is added that the jailor "rejoiced, believing in God, with all his house." Surely when the Bible is so explicit, we ought either to be infidels, or yield to the truth. That my readers may see, however, the incurableness of even good men, when afflicted with a chronic theological disease, I will here give the argument of Dr. Kurtz, which, I really think, he, himself, cannot read, without finding his gravity somewhat disconcerted.

First, Dr. Kurtz says: "*From all we can learn, the jailor was in the prime of life. We are informed that he drew his sword, and would have killed himself, which is not an act characteristic of age, but of a fervid mind and a hasty temper. Again, he called for lights and sprang in; which, in the original, expresses the vigorous action of a strong and robust body,—the vehement burst of an individual full of strength.*" This is to prove that our jailor was a brave, blithe, buxom swain, with his infants all around him. But what an argument! Let us see. The sacred historian tells us there was an earthquake, which wrenched open all the doors in the prison, and thus set the prisoners at liberty; and that the jailor, "supposing the prisoners had been fled, drew his sword, and would have killed himself;" that is, the utter ruin, the certain and ignominious capital punishment which would fall upon him, threw him into despair, and he was on the point of committing suicide. This, says Dr. Kurtz, shews that he "*was in the prime of life!*" The historian adds, that when the jailor found the prisoners all safe, "he called for a light, and sprang in," (*eisepedese* —"*came quickly in.*" In Acts, xiv. 14—*exepedesan*, a stronger word, as Bloomfield remarks, is translated "*ran in*") "and came trembling, and fell down before Paul and Silas." This, Dr. Kurtz affirms, was "*the vehement burst of an individual, full of strength*"*!!* Moreover, it is said, "He was baptized, and ALL HIS straightway;" that is, says Dr. Kurtz, "*he and his numerous family*"*!!!* So that, with Dr. Kurtz, the expression "a man and all his family," means a man with a numerous family. If a man have a large number of children, Dr. Kurtz will allow that they are all his own, and constitute all his children. But if a man have only a few children, Dr. Kurtz will not permit you to speak of him and all his children; for either they are not all his own, or they are not all that he has!!!

Let us go on. The account informs us that "They spake unto him the word of the Lord, and to *all that were in his house.*" Now, whether the jailor had any or many children, I know not; but it is certain, if all in his house heard the word, then there were no infants in the house.

INFANT BAPTISM. 137

Dr. Kurtz professes to be a Greek scholar; if he be, he ought not to have perplexed a plain thing by his false criticisms on the original words rendered "house" in this history. The Greek term for house is *Oikos*, or *Oikia;* each meaning *house*,—each used figuratively to signify *those who dwell in a house;* and our English Bible, with correctness, gives the word *house* as the translation of both. But Dr. Kurtz asserts, without any attempt at proof, that the translation is incorrect. He says that *Oikia* means all in the house; but *Oikos* means strictly *the family*—" children, or children in connection with their parents." To refute this, it is enough to open any Greek Lexicon, or any Greek author; but I will not go out of the Bible. We all know the office which was assigned to Joseph by Pharaoh. He was set over the king's fiscal affairs, and his household establishment. Yet in Acts, vii. 10, it is said by the same writer who records the cases of household baptism, that Joseph was set over Pharoah's house (*oikos*.) "Made him governor over Egypt, and all his house;" that is, according to Dr. Kurtz, made him nurse to his "numerous family of children"!!*

* By reversing Dr. Kurtz's Greek criticisms, one will generally arrive at the truth. Thus he affirms that Baptizo is less emphatic than Bapto; we have seen, in the first part of this essay, that the reverse is true. So in the present instance. He spends page after page reiterating that *Oikia* means the household, *Oikos*, the family; and he draws the picture of a house to reinforce his assertions. Donegan's Lexicon will truly inform those who consult it, that Dr. Kurtz is again with curious infelicity, exactly wrong. *Okios* means "house," "chamber," "household." *Oikia* means house, "*but especially the family.*"

Even, however, by his own criticism, this author refutes himself without seeing it. He affirms that *Oikia* comprehends all who live under the same roof, including the family. Now, it is said, that Paul and Silas preached the word to the jailor, and "to all that were in his house" (*Oikia*.) According to Dr. Kurtz himself, then, all the family were assembled at midnight, and heard the sermon. The sword of Herod was not more fatal to infants than is this criticism of Dr. Kurtz; yet he affirms that this "renders it in his view certain that there were infants"!!!

I proceed. "*The only apparent difficulty that remains,*" says Dr. Kurtz, "*is contained in the assertion that, ' he and all his family rejoiced.' But may there not be infants in the family that rejoices? Nay, may not young children themselves of four or five years of age rejoice? Do we not read: ' out of the mouths of babes and sucklings, thou hast perfected praise?' 'Allow,'* says D. Isaac, *' that the children were baptized on the ground of the father's faith, and all the mystery and difficulty of the passage vanish at once.'*" What shall we say to this? In the first place, when Dr. Kurtz asserts that a whole house may be properly said to rejoice, although there are infants who cannot rejoice, does he not perceive that his argument explodes in his hands, and is fatal to his whole system? For with the same accuracy, of course, a whole family may be said to be baptized, although there be infants who are not baptized. If this will not do, his readers are furnished with another refuge. "*May not young children themselves of four or five years of age rejoice? Do we not read, 'Out of the mouth of babes,'" &c?* So that, after all, Dr. Kurtz's babes are old enough to know spiritual joy, and to utter praises to God! Such infants as these I shall be happy to baptize every day of my life. Ah, my dear brother, allow God's word to triumph over prejudice, and you will not have to call in D. Isaac, or the silly "Editor of Calmet," to help you out of "mystery and difficulty." No mystery, no difficulty whatever will exist.

The most serious complaint I have to make against Dr. Kurtz's argument in this case is still to come. On almost every page of this writer's work I grieve to find words whose virulence, I am sure, do injustice to his heart. "*Difficulty in suppressing indignation at witnessing such a shallow subterfuge ;*" "*tissue of wretched fictions and pitiful shifts ;*"—these are not handsome things to say of any people professing Christianity, yet Dr. Kurtz's pages are stained every now and then with many such things. But let this pass. I repel the idea that the author designed any garbling of God's word; he has, however, omitted that which is at once conclusive in the case of the jailor. The Bible declares that the whole family "*believed;*" "He set meat before them, and rejoiced, believing in God with all his house." Doddridge thus renders it: "Believing in God with all his house, he was even transported with unutterable joy." Dr. Kurtz spoke of the joy, but he omits the express declaration of God that all the house believed.

Matthew Henry.—" The voice of rejoicing, with that of salvation, was heard in the jailor's house,—' He rejoiced, believing in God with all his house;' there was none in his house that refused to be baptized, and so make a jar in the ceremony, but they were unanimous in embracing the gospel, which added much to the joy." Expos. on the place.

Calvin.—" Luke commends the pious zeal of the jailor, because he dedicated his whole house to the Lord; in which, also, the grace of God illustriously appeared, because it suddenly brought the whole family to a pious consent." Comment. in loco.

The only remaining household baptism is that of Lydia's house, and I submit to every candid mind, whether any argument from me ought to be required in this case.

First, when it is said that " she was baptized and her household," what possible inference can be drawn, by either party, from this statement? The question still is, were there any children in this household? and if there were children, were any of them infants? Dr. Miller writes thus: " Was it ever known that a case of family baptism occurred under the direction of a Baptist minister?" " There is no risk in asserting that such a case was never heard of." Dr. Kurtz re-echoes this question and assertion, and an apology for both of them is to be found in their utter ignorance of all that concerns the Baptists. It would be difficult to find any Baptist minister who has been much in revivals without baptizing families. The writer of these pages has baptized several; twice already has he baptized families in Baltimore. " Mr. Smith and all his house are sick;" does this determine anything as to the character, or age, of the persons in Mr. Smith's house? Looking merely to the fact recorded, neither we nor our opponents can take anything by it.

In the next place, the same inspired writer constantly employs the word "*house*" and "*household*" (Oikos,) when all admit there were no infants. In the cases of Cornelius, and Crispus, the jailor, and Stephanas, the same word is used.

Thirdly, the Commission requires faith before baptism, and we have seen that under the Commission the apostles baptized only believers. If, therefore, it had been said that Lydia was married and had children, this case would only resemble that of Stephanas or the jailor.

But, fourthly, there is not a shadow of evidence, either as to her maternity or marriage. From the history it appears that she was a sole-dealer, " a woman of the city of Thyatira," who was at Philippi "selling purple." Not a word is said of her husband or children. Her carrying on business for herself is presumptive against her being married. If married, had she any children? If she had children, were any of them infants? if so, would we not have heard of her husband? If she had an infant, was it with her on this journey by sea and land of not less than 300 miles? Any one of these questions demolishes the whole argument of our opponents. They must prove that Lydia was married, had young children, brought them with her, and that the apostles violated the Commission and departed from their uniform practice in this single instance.

I will only add (though it is quite unnecessary,) that Lydia's address, "If ye have judged me faithful to the Lord come into my house and abide there," is plainly the language of a single woman at the head of her own establishment; and that, afterwards, when Paul and Silas had been released from jail, it is said, "they entered into the house of Lydia, and when they had seen the brethren they comforted them and departed." Leaving the jailor's house, the only other Christian house in the city was that of Lydia; and her "household" were the only other baptized persons. These persons are expressly declared to have been "brethren," whom the apostles saw and comforted.

Mr. Whitby seems to consider this unquestionable. "And when she, and those of her household, were instructed in the Christian faith, in the nature of baptism required by it, she was baptized and her household." Paraphrase on the place.

Assembly of Divines.—"Of the city of Thyatira—a city of Asia—here dwelt Lydia, that devout servant of God." "And entered into the house of Lydia; doubtless to confirm them in the faith which they had preached to them. Lydia and hers hearing of their miraculous deliverance, could not but be comforted and confirmed in the truth." Annot. on Acts, xvi. 14, 40.

CHAPTER III.

From the examples of baptism, I pass now to the references made in the Scripture to the persons baptized. These shew that the subjects were not infants.

In Rom. vi. 3, and Coloss. ii. 12, the subjects are said to be " buried by baptism unto death, that like as Christ was raised up from the dead, so they also should walk in newness of life;" to be " buried with Christ in baptism wherein also they are risen with him through the faith of the operation of God." This is affirmed of all who are baptized, and excludes the idea of unconscious infants.

In 1 Peter, iii. 21, baptism is declared to be " the answer of a good conscience towards God." This, again, is said of all who are baptized; but the conscience of an infant has nothing to do with its baptism. There is, there can be, no answer of conscience as to the act, much less that inward approbation which follows obedience, and to which the apostle alludes.

In Heb. x. 22, we are said to have " our hearts sprinkled from an evil conscience and our bodies washed with (in) pure water." Professor Stuart says, "The Jews were sprinkled with blood that they might be purified so as to have access to God; Christians are internally sprinkled, i. e. purified by the blood of Jesus. The Jews were washed with water in order to be ceremonially purified, so as to come before God; Christians have been washed by the purifying water of baptism." (Com. on Heb.) All this supposes, of course, that baptism is only administered to believers.

Lastly, Gal. iii. 27.—"For as many of you as have been baptized into Christ have put on Christ." Here it is expressly declared that those who are baptized "put on Christ"—a military metaphor borrowed from the uniform which soldiers put on after enlisting. How can this apply to infants?

CHAPTER IV

There is one thought which, to my mind, is of itself conclusive as to the baptism of children. It is this: If it be a duty at all, it is, of course, the duty of the parent. But, while the New Testament is full and minute in giving commands to parents as to their obligations, there is no precept, no insinuation of a precept, as to the duty of baptizing children.

Open the works of our Pædopaptist brethren: how many pages, how many essays, enjoining the duty of bringing children to the font. Now open the Bible. This Bible is the revelation of God's will to man. It is "given by inspiration that the man of God may be perfect, thoroughly furnished unto all good works." In this Bible, God over and over specifies the duties of parents to their children, and enforces those duties by every variety of appeal; yet not an intimation is breathed as to baptizing children! Will any one, after this, pretend that it is required by God?

It is just nothing to say, that the Jews were accustomed to circumcise their children, and would therefore naturally baptize them. I shall hereafter shew that the converted Jews continued to circumcise their children during the apostlic age, so that even as to them this pretext fails. But the New Testament is God's directory for all nations, Gentiles as well as Jews. Yet in this directory not a word is uttered, not a hint given, as to the obligation on parents to baptize their children. What do I say? Not a word uttered? There is a word uttered; that word is the Commission, which directly limits baptism to believers, and thus forbids it to infants. It really does seem to me that this single truth ought to settle this question. And when I add to this the arguments already urged, I feel that if infant baptism be still adhered to, it is not because the word of God is not abundantly clear—it is because the prejudices of birth and education, because old ancestral sanctities, because pride of opinion and long cherished idols of the mind, have a portentous power to bind a bandage over the intellectual vision of some of the best and noblest of mankind.

That this bandage will much longer blind so many of the excellent of the earth I will never believe. Within the last year no less than twenty ministers have renounced this error, and among them are some of the purest and best men. Other true spirits will follow, and emancipate themselves from the skin and film of an obsolete and corrupt theology. Infant dedication ought to be practised, and will be practised; but infant baptism ought to be given up, and will be given up. The apostles said, they "could do nothing against the truth," and the truth on this subject is too manifest for any subtilty, or sophistry, or subterfuge. At least, if any one deems me too sanguine in my anticipations, let him read what follows. Let him ponder the subjoined remarkable concessions from the most able and learned Pædobaptists, and then decide for himself, how long a cause can be defended, when its very apologists thus surrender it.

Dr. Woods says: "We have no express precept or example for infant baptism in all our holy writings." Prof. Stuart admits that he cannot "find commands or plain and certain examples in the New Testament relative to it" (infant baptism.)

These concessions, however, are unimportant, when compared with those made by the most profound and illustrious theological writers the world has ever known. Would that our baptismal essayists possessed half the learning, and all the frankness of these scholars whose whole lives have been devoted to the most laborious ecclesiastical researches. The entire world acknowledges and admires the vast superiority of these German professors in all erudition; and, as is ever the case, true knowledge elevates them above the littleness of prejudice and party, and inspires them with a candor even more admirable than their intellectual wealth. Such are the writers on Baptism in Germany. In this country . . . . . . but I stop, I check myself, and finish this chapter with the underwritten quotations.

Schleiermacher (Christian Theology, p. 383.)—"All traces of infant baptism, which one will find in the New Testament, must first be put into it." "It is a departure from the original institution." "Our symbolical books (that is, the creeds) treat of it without regard to history, and attempt to justify it in itself; but the manner in which they do it is unsatisfactory, and upon grounds that essentially destroy each other."

Prof. Hahn's Theology, p. 556.—"According to its true original design, it can be given only to adults, who are capable of true knowledge, repentance and faith. Neither in the Scriptures, nor during the first hundred and fifty years, is a sure example of infant baptism to be found; and we must concede that the numerous opposers of it cannot be contradicted on gospel ground." "It arose from false views of original sin, and of the magical power of consecrated water."

Winer's Manuscript Lectures.—"Originally only adults were baptized; but at the end of the second century, in Africa, and in the third century, generally, infant baptism was introduced; and in the fourth century it was theologically maintained by Augustine."

Corrodi, quoted by Dressler, 154.—"At the time of Christ and his disciples, only adults were baptized; therefore, among Christians of the present day, not children, but adults who are capable of professing Christianity, ought to be baptized."

Prof. Lange (on Baptism, p. 101.)—" All attempts to make out infant baptism, from the New Testament, fail. It is totally opposed to the spirit of the apostolic age, and to the fundamental principles of the New Testament."

Again (*Geschichte der Protest.* pp. 34, 5.)—" Would the Protestant Church fulfil and attain to its final destiny, the baptism of new-born children must be abolished. It has sunk down to a mere formality, without any religious meaning for the child, and stands in contradiction to the fundamental doctrines of the Reformers, on the advantage and use of the Sacraments. It cannot, from any point of view, be justified by the Holy Scriptures, and owes its origin as well as its retention by the Reformers, to the antiscriptural and irrational idea, that children, because of original sin, are born under the power of the devil, and exposed to eternal condemnation."

Rheinwald (p. 313.)—" The first traces of infant baptism are found in the Western Church, after the middle of the second century, and it was the subject of controversy in Pro-consular Africa, towards the end of this century. Though its necessity was asserted in Africa and Egypt, in the beginning of the third century, it was, even to the end of the fourth century, by no means universally observed—least of all in the Eastern Church. Notwithstanding the recommendation of it by the fathers, it never became a general ecclesiastical institution, till the age of Augustine."

Dressler (on Baptism, p. 137.)—" The idea of a

Christian nobility is foreign to the Bible. By birth man is only man. According to Paul, a holy pedigree is nothing in religion." And p. 147.—" In the New Testament it is nowhere mentioned that the children of Christian parents were baptized; the consecration, by baptism, always relates to those only whose faith was changed, and who were made acquainted with Christ, and became his disciples." At p. 152.—" The immediate occasion of infant baptism, it cannot be denied, was extravagant ideas of its necessity to salvation. We are not, however, to regard it as worthless and unmeaning, because it was introduced from false views and opinions."

Von Coln, v. i. p. 466.—" Exorcism was practised in early times only with demoniacs; then it became a catechetical preparation; and after infant baptism was introduced, it was a part of the baptismal rite."

Hase's Theology, p. 449.—" Baptism obligates a man to a Christian life; but how can one who is unconcious obligate himself to any thing ?"

Marheinecke's Principles of Theology, p. 344.—" It is superstitious to believe that one is baptized in order to be consecrated to God; for he is rather to be baptized because he is already consecrated to God."

Hutterus Redivivus of 1833, p. 341.—" The imputation of the parents' faith to their children must be laid aside as an opus operatum" (that is, a mere form.)

Klein (quoted in Hutt. Rediv. p. 344.)—" New born infants are incapable of faith; and the New Testament mentions the baptism of adults only."

Baumgarten Crusius, Hist. of Theology, p. 1208.—"Infant baptism can be supported neither by a distinct apostolical tradition, nor apostolical practice."

Starck, Hist. of Bap. p. 11.—"There is not a single example to be found in the New Testament where infants were baptized. In household baptisms, there was always reference to the gospel's having been received. The New Testament presents just as good grounds for infant communion." "The connection of infant baptism with circumcision deserves no consideration, since there were physical reasons for circumcising in infancy."

Kaiser's Bib. Theology, v. 2, p. 178.—"Infant baptism was not an original institution of Christianity. When it is said of Lydia, that she was baptized with her whole house, it evidently means only those who were capable of it, or who believed. In Acts, xviii. 8, it is said that the baptized household had believed. The first traces of infant baptism are in the second century."

Prof. Lindner, of Leipsic (on the Supper, p. 123.)—"Christian baptism can be given only to adults, not to infants. The Holy Spirit, which is given only to believers, was a prerequisite to baptism."

Olshausen, v. 2, p. 454.—"By the introduction of infant baptism, which was certainly not apostolical, the relative position of baptism, after the ebullition of spiritual gifts had passed away, was changed." P. 158—"In infant baptisms, which the church, at a later period, for wise reasons introduced, the sacred rite returned back, as it were, to the inferior rank of John's baptism."

Lastly. Neander (Hist. of Chr. Relig. v. 1, p. 360.)—

"It is certain that Christ did not ordain infant baptism. He left, indeed, much which was not needful for salvation, to the free development of the Christian spirit, without here appointing binding laws. We cannot prove that the apostles ordained infant baptism. From these places where the baptism of a whole family is mentioned, as in Acts, xvi. 33, 1 Cor. i. 16, we can draw no such conclusion, because the inquiry is still to be made, whether there were any children in these families of such an age that they were not capable of any intelligent reception of Christianity, for this is the only point on which the case turns."

Neander's Apostolic Age, v. 1, p. 140.—"The practice of infant baptism was remote from the spirit of this (apostolical) age. From the examples of household baptism, infant baptism can by no means be inferred; for the passage, 1 Cor. xvi. 15, shows the incorrectness of such a conclusion. It is there made evident that the whole family of Stephanas, baptized by Paul, consisted purely of adults. Not only the late appearance of any express mention of infant baptism, but the long continued opposition to it, leads to the conclusion that it was not of apostolical origin."

CHAPTER V.

WE have just seen that even Dr. Woods and Prof. Stuart give up all pretence of either "express precept or example" in the Bible, by which to defend infant baptism ; and, with an unprejudiced mind, this is enough to condemn it. Baptism is a positive institution. Moral duties may be inferred from the fitness of things, or the general law of right and wrong. But the obligation to be immersed in water does not arise from any such consideration; it is created entirely by a special enactment; it is plain, therefore, that every thing concerning baptism must be determined by this special enactment, that is, the Commission.

When our opponents, then, confess that there is neither "express precept nor example," they virtually abandon their whole cause. Do you ask us, Baptists, "By what authority we do these things, and who gave us this authority?" We point you to the Commission, which we, like the apostles, implicitly obey. When, however, this inquiry is made of our Pædobaptist brethren, what is their answer? They acknowledge that they have neither "express precept nor example," but endeavor to sustain themselves by inferences, by remote analogies, by arguments, in short, which (as Schleiermacher, p. 383, confesses) are not only in themselves "unsatisfactory," but which "essentially destroy each other."

They remind one of the Jews, when Jesus demanded of them, "whether the baptism of John was from heaven or of men?" It was a gravelling question that. And just so, when our brethren are required to give the authority for infant baptism. Of course the only authority for any baptism is the Commission; but from that document they turn cautiously away, and, in attempting to justify their error, they not only conflict with God's word, but with each other. "Infants are born members," says one denomination, "and, therefore, ought to be baptized." "That will not do," says another; "natural birth cannot make one a member of the Church. Infants are baptized because they are not members, and in order that they may be 'grafted in.'" Some plead circumcision; others reject this plea, declaring that "circumcision deserves no consideration," and put infant baptism on the ground of "feeling;" this is the defence of even such a man as Niemeyer, v. 1, p. 400. Now, it is the faith of the parent; then, this is ridiculed, and we are told that "the imputation of the faith of the parent must be laid aside as a mere figment." In short, there is no end to these contradictions, and there will be none until our beloved brethren renounce this cherished idol. Until then, however pious and nobly devoted in other things, they will here be involved in hopeless confusion. Infant baptism "bewitches them" that they do not see the truth. They resemble Sampson in the intellectual might and prowess which they bring to other subjects; but on this they present the mournful spectacle exhibited by that hero, when, blinded and shorn of his invincible locks, he groped in darkness, and sought in vain to "shake himself, as was his wont at other times before."

In this chapter I take up the passages of the New Testament, from which it has been attempted to support infant baptism by inference. I have already disposed of the household baptisms. The first passage now to be examined is in Mark, x. 14, where little children were brought unto Christ, and " He took them up in his arms, and put his hands upon them, and blessed them." I have before urged infant dedication from this passage; but what has it do with baptism? Nay, it is conclusive against baptizing infants, for Christ himself here only blesses the children. He was now " making and baptizing disciples ;" yet he neither baptizes the children, nor uttters an intimation as to their being baptized.

But does he not say, " Of such is the kingdom of heaven?" What then? How does this touch baptism? Suppose he had said that infants were of the kingdom of heaven; even this would have nothing to do with their baptism. It would only be saying that infants will be saved, which nobody questions. It is unnecessary, however, to argue this, since Jesus says nothing of the kind. He says, " *of such*," that is, of those who resemble these, " is the kingdom of heaven." Whether the " kingdom of heaven" means, here, the church, or the society of the redeemed in heaven, I need not inquire. One thing is self-evident—" *of such*," is a comparison, and "*simile non est idem*," that which resembles a thing is not the thing itself. The meaning is, " None can enter the kingdom of heaven but those who resemble these children, who are like them in meekness and teachableness." Had the Saviour declared that the kingdom of heaven is " of little children," it would exclude all others, and be equivalent to saying that none but little children can be in the kingdom. But Jesus utters no such monstrous doctrine. He does not say, " The kingdom of heaven is of little children," but of such as resembled little children; not "*of these,*" but "*of such as these.*" When Jesus speaks of those who are in his kingdom, observe how different is the phraseology. "Blessed are the poor in spirit, for *theirs* is the kingdom of heaven;" "Blessed are the pure in heart, for *they* shall see God;" viz: "None but the poor in spirit and pure in heart are members of the kingdom, and shall see God." How different in the passage before us is his language. Here it is not, Blessed are children, for *they* are of the kingdom of heaven, but "*of such* (of those who resemble children) is the kingdom of heaven." In the very next verse he cuts off all cavilling. He there adds, "Verily I say unto you, whosoever shall not receive the kingdom of God as a little child, he shall not enter therein."

This passage plainly makes against infant baptism. Had it been customary to baptize infants, would the disciples have forbidden the parents to bring their children? Do Pædobaptist ministers ever forbid parents to bring their children to the font? Had infant baptism been a duty, would not these parents have sought it from Jesus? and would not some intimation have been given, on so important an occasion, as to this duty? I repeat it, this case recoils fatally against our opponents. The passage conveys, too, a solemn admonition to us all. For, if received with the docility and simplicity of children, the word of God is perfectly plain on many subjects which have caused oceans of ink and rivers of blood to flow.

Barnes (on this passage.)—"The kingdom of heaven evidently means here the church. Whosoever shall not be humble, unambitious and docile, shall not be a true follower of Christ, or a member of his kingdom. Of such as these—that is, of persons with such tempers as these—is the church to be composed. He does not say, of those infants, but of such persons as resemble them, or were like them in temper, was the kingdom of heaven made up." So Kuinöl, Rosenmueller and Bloomfield.

Bishop Taylor.—"From the action of Christ's blessing infants, to infer they are to be baptized, proves nothing so much as that there is a want of better arguments; for the conclusion would with more probability be derived thus: Christ blessed infants, and so dismissed them, but baptized them not; therefore infants are not to be baptized."—Liberty of Prophecy, p. 230.

The next passage which has been violently laid under contribution is in Acts, ii. 39.—"For the promise is unto you and to your children." These words are frequently quoted in this garbled manner; but is not this "handling the word of God deceitfully?" Let us look at the whole passage. "Then Peter said unto them, Repent and be baptized, every one of you, in the name of Jesus Christ, for the remission of sins; and ye shall receive the gift of the Holy Ghost. For the promise is unto you and to your children, and to all that are afar off, even as many as the Lord our God shall call. Then they that gladly received his word were baptized."

Now, what is the promise here mentioned?· At v. 16, 17, we are expessely informed that it was a promise of the miraculous gifts of the Holy Ghost, which of

INFANT BAPTISM. 157

course infants were incapable of receiving. "This is that which is spoken of by the Prophet Joel, *And it shall come to pass in the last days I will pour out my spirit upon all flesh, and your sons and daughters shall prophesy,*" &c. This promise, says Peter, is "*to you* (*Jews*) *and your children;*" viz. "your sons and your daughters," (not infants, which would be absurd, but, as Joel says, "sons and daughters,") *and to all that are afar off,*" (as Joel says, "all flesh," viz. Gentiles who hitherto were aliens,) "*even as many as the Lord our God shall call.*" How preposterous to talk of infants being called.

What renders more strange the fatuity of seeking to enlist this passage in the cause of infant baptism is, that it is conclusive against the practice. For, not only does the clause last quoted exclude infants, but we are told (v. 41) that none were baptized but believers. Three thousand were baptized, yet not even an allusion to an infant. "*Then they that gladly received his word were baptized.*"

Whitby.—"These words will not prove a right of infants to receive baptism; the promise here being that only of the Holy Ghost, mentioned in verses 16, 17, 18, and so relating only to the times of the miraculous effusion of the Holy Ghost, and to those persons, who by age, were capable of these extraordinary gifts." Annot. on the place.

Doddridge.—"'The promise is to you and to your children.' Considering that the gift of the spirit had been mentioned just before, it seems most natural to interpret this as a reference to that passage in Joel, which had been so largely recited above, ver. 17, &c., where God promises the effusion of the spirit on their sons and their daughters." Fam. Expos. Note on the place.

Hammond.—"If any have made use of that very unconcludent argument," (referring to this passage, Acts, ii. 39,) "I have nothing to say in defence of them. The word children there, is really the posterity of the Jews, and not peculiarly their infant children." Works, vol. i. p. 490.

Limborch, a learned divine of Amsterdam.—"By 'children' the apostle means not infants, but posterity; in which signification the word occurs in many places of the New Testament (see among others, John, viii. 39, 'If ye were Abraham's children, ye would do the works of Abraham.') Whence it appears that the argument which is very commonly taken from this passage, for the baptism of infants, is of no force and good for nothing." Comment. in loc.

The last passage which has been subjected to exegetical torture in the hope of extorting something, is 1 Cor. vii. 14. "For the unbelieving husband is sanctified by the wife, and the unbelieving wife is sanctified by the husband, else were your children unclean, but now are they holy." Can the most prejudiced mind, however, find anything about infant baptism here?

Suppose I admit that the word "holy," means morally holy; still, where is the commission to baptize holy children? Christ says, "Go, teach, and baptize." He no more sends us to baptize holy children than holy angels.

But are children morally holy because one parent is a believer? Are children born holy if both parents are Christians? Are our brethren so wedded to infant baptism that, in their efforts to defend it, they will abandon the doctrine of depravity? "Who can bring a clean thing out of an unclean?" "Behold I was shapen in iniquity and in sin did my mother conceive me." "We were by nature all children of wrath." "As by one man sin entered into the world, and death by sin, so death passed upon all men because all have sinned." In fact, we detect here, again, another of the contradictions into which this error betrays its advocates, for, on one page, our brethren declare that infants are baptized on account of original sin; and, on the next, quote this passage and say, they are baptized because they are holy!

To one who studies this Epistle impartially, the passage is not only plain, but the necessity for this counsel is at once seen. It was unlawful for a Jew to marry a Gentile. Hence, when the Jews were called to repent, they were required to put away their Gentile wives. Such marriages are, in Ezra, ch. ix. 2, called, "the holy seed mingling themselves with the people of those lands;" and in ch. x. 11, the holy seed, or Jews, are exhorted to "separate themselves from their strange wives." Among Christians the duty enjoined as to marriage was, that it should be "only in the Lord;" viz. Christians ought not to marry unbelievers. Now, a very serious question would arise, where only one of the parties was a Christian. What should be done? Was it the believer's duty to leave the unbeliever, as by the Jewish rule? It is for this case the apostle is giving directions. He says, the marriage relation should continue; it is still sacred; otherwise, in the sight of God, your offspring would be the fruit of an unholy union. The language does not refer to the legitimacy of the children according to the laws of the land, but to their character in the sight of God. If the union of Christians with unbelievers was like that of Jew with Gentile, not only would cohabitation be criminal, but the children would, in the sight of God, be the children of an improper intercourse. But this was not the case. The gospel recognizes the children as the fruit of holy wedlock. The consciences of Christians, therefore, need not be troubled by supposing that the law of intermarriage between Jew and Gentile applied to these cases.

What exposes utterly the idea of moral holiness in this case is, that the same holiness is ascribed to the "*unbelieving husband and wife.*" "The unbelieving husband is sanctified by the wife, and the unbelieving wife is sanctified by the husband." If the argument of our opponents is good, then it follows, that a husband, though an infidel, and utterly vicious, is sanctified, i. e., perfectly holy, as soon as his wife is converted, and ought to be baptized on the ground of his wife's faith!!

Mr. Barnes says,—"There is not one word about baptism here; nor an allusion to it, nor does the argument in the remotest degree bear upon it."

Mr. T. Williams, of London.—"The unbelieving husband is sanctified by the (believing) wife, &c., so that the connection is perfectly lawful, and the children are legitimate, or, in a ceremonial sense, holy." Cottage Bible on the place.

Melancthon.—"The connexion of the argument is this, 'If the use of marriage does not please God, your children would be bastards and so unclean; but your children are not bastards, therefore the use of marriage pleaseth God.' How bastards were unclean in a peculiar manner the law shows, Deut. xxiii." In Pædobap. Exam. vol. ii. p. 375.

Dr. Macknight.—"I therefore, think with Elsner, that the words in this verse have neither a federal nor a moral meaning, but are used in the idiom of the Hebrews," &c. Translation of the Apost. Epist. Note on 1 Cor. vii. 14.

Dressler, in his Doctrine of the Sacrament of Baptism, published 1830, p. 137.—"The idea of a Christian nobility is foreign to the Bible. By birth, man is only man. According to Paul, a holy pedigree is nothing in religion. Neither circumcision nor uncircumcision availeth anything, but keeping the commands of God. The passage, 1 Cor. vii. 13, does not support any such views. Paul had said that if one would avoid all contact with pagans, he must leave the world. He now says, if the Corinthians would flee from every unbeliever, regarding him as unclean, they must flee from their own children, and hold them as unclean: for they were among the unbelievers—'otherwise your children would be unclean,' for they are not Christians by birth merely. 'But now are they holy,' i. e. you are not to consider yourselves as polluted by them."

CHAPTER VI.

I HAVE thus examined the question before us as far as the New Testament is concerned; and is not the New Testament the sole and ultimate arbiter in this matter? Is not baptism entirly a New Testament institution? and is it not monstrous to go into the Old Testament to see who are to be baptized? Into the Old Testament, however, our opponents go; and there I must now follow them.

For, although the very attempt to find infant baptism in the Old Testament would strike any unprejudiced mind as utterly preposterous, yet, in this way, many persons are bewildered and "turned away from the truth." It is not surprising that the sophistries drawn from this source, have, with multitudes, the semblance and force of argument. They are excited and anxious to be confirmed in their views; the smallest gleam of light, therefore, dazzles them, and causes them to welcome, as truth, the grossest illusions.

The first plea from the Old Testament is built upon the Abrahamic covenant, and this plea virtually includes all other pleas from this quarter. Now, as to this plea, I submit to every candid mind a single reflection, which ought to supersede the necessity of discussion. I ask, can infant baptism be a duty commanded by God; and yet the world be left "without command or example," and plain men be required to discover this duty in the mists and mazes, where the most learned lose themselves as soon as they attempt to find infant baptism in the covenant of circumcision? Baptism is for all nations. The Gentiles knew nothing about this covenant. Were they, as well as the Jews, to travel out of the only Commission authorizing baptism, and to detect their duty to God and their children, by these metaphysical subtilties and forced analogies?

The argument from this covenant may be thus stated. In the Old Testament God covenanted with Abraham and his seed. Circumcision was the seal of that covenant. This covenant extends to parents and their children now. Baptism is the seal of this covenant, having come in the place of circumcision. Such is the argument. But I implore my brethren calmly to look at this reasoning, before they abolish the baptism of the Commission, by a baptism thus fetched in by assumptions utterly forbidden by the Bible.

In the first place, what did God promise to Abraham? Truth requires me to differ from those Baptists who deny that there is any spiritual import in these promises. There is plainly a spirit and a letter. Spiritually the promises are these:—(1) That Christ should spring from Abraham, and that he should thus be the father of the faithful. "Now to Abraham and his *seed* were the promises made. He saith not, *and to seeds*, as of many, but as of one. And to thy *seed*, which is Christ." (Gal. iii. 16.) (2) The second spiritual promise was, that in Abraham "all nations should be blessed;" viz: as Abraham's faith was counted to him for righteousness, so all, in every nation, who believe, shall inherit the same blessing, and have their faith accounted for righteousness. "He received the sign of circumcision, a seal of the righteousness of the faith which he had, being yet uncircumcised; that he might be the father of all them that believe, though they be not circumcised, (*viz. the Gentiles*,) that righteousness might be imputed unto them also; and the father of circumcision (i. e. might bequeath the spiritual blessings of the covenant) to them who are not of the circumcision only, (*not only Jews outwardly*,) but who also walk in the steps of that faith of our father Abraham which he had, being yet uncircumcised." So, then, they which be of faith (*Jews or Gentiles*) are blessed with faithful Abraham;" viz: the spiritual blessing is, that faith, wherever found, is imputed for righteousness. "And if ye be Christ's, then are ye Abraham's seed, and heirs according to the promise;" viz: your faith, like Abraham's faith, secures spiritual blessings, by uniting the soul to Christ. (Rom. iv. 11, 12, Gal. iii. 9, 29.) (3) The last spiritual blessing was, that, in a glorious sense, God would be a God to those who were thus by faith the children of Abraham. A promise this more fully expressed in Jer. xxxi. 33. "But this shall be the covenant that I will make with the house of Israel after those days, saith the Lord; I will put my law in their inward parts, and write it in their hearts; and I will be their God, and they shall be my people."

Now, it is self-evident that circumcision was no seal of these spiritual blessings. For, in the first place, the blessings are only to those who have the faith of Abraham. But **infants cannot have faith.** In the next place, circumcision was performed upon slaves simply on the ground of property. "He that is bought with thy money must be circumcised." A Jew who bought slaves was compelled by the covenant to circumcise them at once, without any reference to their character, and simply because they were his property. Thirdly, Ishmael was expressly excluded from the spiritual promises, yet he was circumcised. Fourthly, the spiritual blessings were for all who should have faith, of all nations, and of each sex; circumcision was restricted to the males of the Jewish nation.

The temporal promises of the Abrahamic covenant were, a numerous posterity to Abraham; the theocracy or special government of God in leading and defending the nation; and (above all) the land of Canaan.

Such is the Abrahamic covenant. Now I ask any candid reader, what has this to do with baptism? Had not men a system to defend, and were not people's minds confounded with a jargon about "covenant mercies," no one could receive so many errors as are united in this argument. There are no less than five fallacies in this plea, any one of which need only be indicated to expose the utter sophistry of the whole thing.

(1.) The first error is, *that the covenant with Abraham is the covenant of redemption by which men are saved.* The covenant of salvation was with Christ from eternity. By this he undertook to die and make atonement for our sins. All who have faith in Christ are partakers in the blessings of this covenant of his blood. And though God has not sent a revelation to infants, which would be absurd, yet "Christ is set forth to be a propitiation for the sins of the whole world," and infants are saved through that propitiation. How monstrous to confound this glorious covenant, with the special transaction between God and the Patriarch of the Jewish nation.

(2.) The second error is, *that circumcision was a seal of spiritual blessings to Abraham's natural offspring.* The Bible indeed calls circumcision "a seal," but to whom, and of what? To Abraham alone; and of "the righteousness of faith which he had, being yet uncircumcised." That is to say, the institution of this badge was an assurance and signature by God to Abraham, that he was accepted, and that on account of his piety a marked distinction should be conferred on him and his heirs. It was a sign to him, just as the rainbow was to Noah "a token" of God's covenant with him.— Gen. ix. 13.

Circumcision is never called a seal to any one but Abraham; and I have already shown it was no badge of spiritual blessings.

(3.) *Suppose, however, this covenant had ensured spiritual blessings to Abraham's posterity, how can we insert ourselves into it?* Here is a third error.. We have seen that in its *spiritual import* the covenant was with Abraham as the father of those who have faith. All, therefore, of every nation, who believe, are Abraham's spiritual children, and thus the promise is to them that their faith shall be imputed for righteousness. But circumcision was only for Abraham's carnal offspring, and as far as the covenant concerned them, it was plainly confined to them. A king, in consideration of the loyalty of a subject, confers a title, with a peculiar mark, on that subject and all his posterity; how absurd it would be for all the subjects to argue, that they and their children were included in the grant. Just so here. God made a covenant with Abraham and his household; therefore, God makes the same covenant with every Christian and his household! Why, with as much reason, might every Englishman reason thus: By the constitution of Great Britain, Victoria is queen, and her eldest son heir of the throne; therefore, by the same constitution, I am king, and my eldest son is heir to the throne. The covenant with Abraham is a peculiar transaction with him. I will here recite it, and I ask any Christian parent, has God made this covenant with you? Has he promised you, that you shall be the parent of kings? that you shall have a numerous posterity? and that you shall possess the land of Canaan? It is really astonishing that people have been so long imposed on in this matter.

"*And when Abram was ninety years old and nine, the Lord appeared to Abram, and said unto him, I am the Almighty God; walk before me and be thou perfect. And I will make my covenant between me and thee, and will multiply thee exceedingly. And Abram fell on his face; and God talked with him saying, As for me, behold my covenant is with thee, and thou shalt be a father of many nations. Neither shall thy name be any more called Abram, but thy name shall be called Abraham; for a father of many nations have I made thee. And I will make thee exceedingly fruitful, and I will make nations of thee, and kings shall come out of thee. And I will establish my covenant between me and thee, and thy seed after thee in their generations, for an everlasting covenant to be a God unto thee, and to thy seed after thee. And I will give unto thee, and to thy seed after thee, the land wherein thou art a stranger, all the land of Canaan, for an everlasting possession; and I will be their God. And God said unto Abraham, Thou shalt keep my covenant, therefore, thou, and thy seed after thee, in their generations. This is my covenant, which ye shall keep, between me and you and thy seed after thee: Every man child among you shall be circumcised. And you shall circumcise the flesh of your foreskin: and it shall be a token of the covenent betwixt me and you. And he that is eight days old shall be circumcised among you, every man child in your generations, he that is born in the house, or bought with money of any stranger, which is not of thy seed. He that is born in the house, and he that is bought with thy money, must needs be circumcised."*

(4.) A fourth error is, *that baptism is a seal of something.* Baptism is an act of obedience, by which we put on and publicly confess Christ. It is emblematical of his death and resurrection, and of our being dead unto sin and alive unto righteousness. It is never represented in the Bible as a seal. The Gospel seal is not water, but the Holy Spirit, " by whom believers are sealed unto the day of redemption." "In whom ye also trusted, after that ye heard the word of truth, the gospel of your salvation. In whom, also, after that ye believed, ye were sealed with that Holy Spirit of promise." (Eph. i. 13.) I do adjure my brethren no longer to speak of baptism as being the seal of the Gospel. The phrase, "*sealing ordinance*," is not in the vocabulary of Christ; it is a part of that deplorable and pernicious language of Ashdod, invented in other days for the defence of infant baptism, and which now serves to pervert the Gospel in the minds of multitudes. To sprinkle water on a child and call it God's seal, is Puseyism, no matter who does it.

(5.) Lastly, the whole argument from the Abrahamic covenant rests upon the assumption that *baptism is in the place of circumcision.* But never was there a supposition more gratuitous and false. With as much reason might it be pretended that baptism came in room of the rainbow, which was the sign of God's covenant with Noah.

Look at the command to circumcise. "He that is eight days old shall be circumcised among you, every male child in your generations, he that is born in the house, or bought with money of any stranger." Now open the Commission. "Go teach all nations, baptizing them," &c. "Go preach the Gospel to every creature, he that believeth, and is baptized," &c. Is that a sane mind which affirms that the latter command is in the room of the former?

In the next place, circumcision was a distinct, positive institution; baptism is also a distinct, positive institution. By what authority shall any mortal dare to abrogate one, and put the other in its stead?

Thirdly, were ever two institutions more unlike? Circumcision was for one sex; baptism for both. Circumcision was on the eighth day; baptism after believing. Parents circumcised their own children; do they baptize their own children? Adults circumcised themselves; do they baptize themselves? Slaves were circumcised on the ground of property. A Jew was required to put this mark on his slave, and to use force if he resisted. Is this the law of Christian baptism? Neither faith nor any moral qualification was required of adults before they were circumcised. The Shechemites (Gen. xxxiv.) were circumcised that they might intermarry with the Israelites. Would our brethren baptize a young man that he might marry a lady in their churches? Do they not require faith in adults? In short, circumcision was a parental duty, the command was to the parent; baptism is a personal duty, and the command to each individual for himself.

A man who, with the above arguments before him, can still maintain that baptism has come in the room of circumcision, might well be pronounced inaccessible to conviction. But there is one fact which must convince even such a man. It is, that *circumcision continued to be practised by the converted Jews during the whole of the apostolical age;* a fact this which is conclusive, and of which we have the most ample testimony. Neander confesses that this settles the point, and asks, how could infant baptism be put in the place of "the circumcision which continued to be practised by the Jewish Christians?" "In that case," he adds, "the dispute carried on with the Judaizing party, on the necessity of circumcision" (viz. for the Gentiles,) "would easily have given an opportunity of introducing this substitute into the controversy." *

That neither John nor Christ regarded baptism as a substitute for circumcision, is certain. The multitude baptized by John and by Christ, had all been previously circumcised. Christ's apostles, then, before his death, knew nothing of this plea. After his death they were regulated by the Commission. Does the Commission say anything about regarding baptism as in the room of circumcision? Does it not forbid any such idea? And the entire practice of the apostles proves that such a thought never entered into their minds.

In Acts xv. we find some of the preachers from Jerusalem requiring the Gentiles to be circumcised. Could this have been possible if baptism had come in the room of circumcision? This requisition gave rise to a great controversy, to settle which the inspired apostles met in council. Now if Christ had established baptism in the room of circumcision, could it have been necessary to hold this council to "consider of this matter?" In short, what is the decision of this council? As Neander says, if baptism had come in the place of circumcision, of course the apostles would now have said so, and thus have promptly settled the controversy. But they intimate nothing of the kind. They simply declare that God does not require circumcision of the Gentiles; that is, it was a rite confined to the Jews.

In Acts xvi. we find that Paul circumcised Timothy,

* Planting and Training of Ch. Book iii. ch. v.

his mother being a Jewess. Paul did this on account of the strong feeling among the Jewish Christians, which Timothy would have to encounter as a preacher, if he were not circumcised. This was some time after Timothy's conversion and baptism (v. 1.) How conclusive this, that circumcision was not superseded.

In fine, not only was circumcision not superseded, but such a sentiment was regarded as a flagrant heresy by the apostles. In Acts xxi. this was the charge brought against Paul on his return to Jerusalem. There was a rumor, that he had propagated false doctrine, teaching the Jews that circumcision had ceased. Of course, this accusation could never have been made if circumcision had ceased. And what is his defence? Does he plead that baptism was a substitute for the Jewish rite? No. He repels the charge as a calumny, and takes measures to satisfy the Jews of his innocence.

"And when they heard it, they glorified the Lord; and said unto him, Thou seest, brother, how many thousands of Jews there are which believe; and they are all zealous of the law. And they are informed of thee, that thou teachest all the Jews which are among the Gentiles to forsake Moses, saying *that they ought not to circumcise their children*, neither to walk after the customs. What is it therefore? The multitude must needs come together: for they will hear that thou art come. Do therefore this that we say to thee. We have four men which have a vow on them. Them take, and purify thyself with them, and be at charges with them, that they may shave their heads: and all may know that those things, whereof they were informed concerning thee are nothing, but that thou thyself also walkest orderly, and keepest the law. *As touching the Gentiles which believe*, we have written and concluded that they observe no such things, save only that they keep themselves from things offered to idols, and from blood, and from strangled, and from fornication. Then Paul took the men; and the next day purifying himself with them, entered into the temple to signify the accomplishment of the days of purification, until an offering should be offered for every one of them."

After this, can any man pretend that baptism has come in the room of circumcision? But if it has not, the whole argument from the Abrahamic covenant falls to the ground.

Venema (see Pæd. Exam. v. 2, p. 268.)—"Circumcision was a seal of the righteousness of faith, as the apostle affirms; but this only in respect of such Israelites as were believers.

Charnock (v. 2, p. 781.)—"God seals no more than he promises. He promises only to faith, and, therefore, only seals to faith. Covenant graces, therefore, must be possessed and acted, before covenant blessings be ratified to us."

Starck, Hist. of Bap. p. 11.—"There is not a single example to be found in the New Testament where infants were baptized. In household baptism, there was always reference to the gospel's having been received. The New Testament presents just as good grounds for infant communion. Therefore, learned men (such as Salmasius, Arnold, Louis de Vives, Suicer, and W. Strabo,) have regarded both infant baptism and infant communion as an innovation introduced since the apostolic times. The connection of infant baptism with circumcision, deserves no consideration, since there were physical reasons for circumcising in infancy.

Augusti, 7, p. 329.—"The parallel between circumcision and baptism is altogether foreign to the New Testament." Prof. Lange, speaking on this point, says, this comparison is without foundation, because "the only circumcision of the gospel dispensation, is, according to Paul, that of the heart."

Paullus, in his Commentary.—"The parallel of circumcision with baptism is inapposite; for by circumcision, one was received into the nation as such, not to a religious faith."

Neander (Plant. and Tr. of Ch. p. 102.)—"If we wish to ascertain from whom this institution (infant baptism) was originated, we should say, certainly not immediately from Christ himself. Was it from the primitive church in Palestine, from an injunction given by the earlier apostles? But among the Jewish Christians circumcision was held as a seal of the covenant, and hence they had so much less occasion to make use of another dedication for their children. Could it then have been Paul, who first, among heathen Christians, introduced this alteration by the use of baptism? But this would agree least of all with the peculiar characteristics of this apostle. He who says of himself that "Christ sent him not to baptize, but to preach the gospel;" he who always kept his eyes fixed on one thing, justification by faith, and so carefully avoided every thing which could give a handle or support to the notion of a justification by outward things, how could he have set up infant baptism against the circumcision that continued to be practised by the Jewish Christians? In this case, the dispute carried on with the Judaizing party, as to the necessity of circumcision, would easily have given an opportunity of introducing this substitute into the controversy, if it had really existed.

Prof. Stuart (on Old Testament, ch. 22.)—"How unwary, too, are many excellent men, in contending for infant baptism, on the ground of the Jewish analogy of circumcision! Are females not proper subjects of baptism? And again, are a man's slaves to be all baptized because he is? Are they church-members of course, when they are so baptized? Is there no difference between engrafting into a politico-ecclesiastical community, and into one of which it is said, that it is not of this world? In short, numberless difficulties present themselves in our way, as soon as we begin to argue in such a manner as this."

CHAPTER VII.

ANOTHER plea for infant baptism, from the Old Testament, nearly resembles that just exposed, and rests on the same false premises and assumptions. The argument is this. The Christian Church is a continuation of the Jewish Church. Infants were members of the Jewish Church; therefore infants are members of the Christian Church. Baptism has come in the room of circumcision; therefore infants ought to be baptized.

If I should grant the "sameness of the Christian and Jewish Churches," what would follow? Not that infants are to be baptized, but that they are to be circumcised. For, after the last chapter, I am unwilling to believe that any one will affirm that baptism has come in the room of circumcision. This is enough to dispose of this plea. As this pretext, however, has, at times, bewildered many, it is worth a moment's attention.

When urging the covenant of circumcision, our opponents call baptism the *seal*. In the present argument they call it the *door*. They tell us it is "the door to the visible church;" an assertion which contains almost as many errors as words. Baptism is never represented in the Bible as a door. It is no more a door than it is a window or a chimney. Baptism is an act of personal obedience, by which a believer publicly confesses Christ. It does not initiate any body into any church.

Let me make this plain. And, for this purpose, let me remark that the Greek word translated "church," means simply "an assembly." (*Ekklesia*, from *Ek-kaleo*, to call forth.) It is applied, in Acts, xix. 32, to a mob. "Some, therefore, cried one thing, and some another, for the assembly (*Ekklesia*) was confused." In the same large sense it is applied to the Jewish nation in Acts, vii.

38. "This is he that was in the church (*Ekklesia*) in the wilderness." It should have been, "in the nation, or congregation of Israel, in the wilderness."

As designating a religious body, the word has, in the Bible, only two senses. It means either the whole company of the regenerated, or a particular society combined for religious purposes. If you inquire who is qualified to be received into a Christian Church properly organized, the answer is easy. The Bible requires repentance, faith, and baptism. These are the qualifications. One thus qualified is received by the church which he desires to join, and is, thus, initiated by the voice of the members. It is gross usurpation in priests or ministers to deprive the church of this right, and to monopolize it themselves. It is manifest, too, that the act of baptism does not make one a member of any church. Not of the spiritual body of the regenerated, for many are baptized who are not regenerated; and not of any one of the particular societies, for, as in the case of the Eunuch, a man may be baptized away from these societies.

Baptism is, indeed, one of the prerequisites to membership in any of the visible churches, and in our churches the candidate generally comes before the church previously to his baptism, because this saves the trouble of a subsequent examination. But a minister may baptize, as Philip did, without consulting any church. It his work, and not that of the church.

With these remarks, let us look now at the argument before us. When it is affirmed that the Christian

Church and the Jewish Church are the same, what is meant by the word "church?" Is it the truly regenerated? If so, I agree with our opponents. Those who repent and believe, whether Jew or Greek, bond or free, are members of the same spiritual body, and ought to be baptized.

This however, is not what our opponents mean by the Jewish Church. They mean Jewish parents with their families; that is, the Jewish nation. But can anything be more glaring than the assertion, that the Christian Church is a continuation of the Jewish nation? Jesus said to his disciples, whom he had called out of the *Jewish nation,* "I have chosen you out of the *world.*" He calls the Jewish nation "the world." Is the Christian Church the same as the world? Not only children, but slaves, (and because they had been purchased,) were members of the Jewish nation. If a man belong to a Christian Church, are all his children and all his slaves members too? Nicodemus was a distinguished member of the Jewish nation. When Jesus told him that unless he was born again he could not be a member of his church, did he mean that he could not be a member of the Jewish nation? The Shechemites were admitted into the Jewish nation simply because they desired wives among the Israelites. Do our brethren admit members into their churches on this ground? The leaders of the Jewish nation persecuted and crucified the Redeemer. Is the Church of that Redeemer the same with the nation of which those murderers were the chiefs? In fine, it is said of Saul, that he "made havoc of the church." He himself thus spake, "Ye have heard of my conduct, in the times past, in the Jews' religion, how that, beyond measure, I persecuted the Church of God." Was it the Jewish nation that he persecuted?

I will not affront the common sense of my readers by supposing that farther argument is necessary on this matter. This whole plea rests on four palpable fallacies.

It takes for granted that circumcision was a seal of spiritual blessings to all who were circumcised, which I have shewn to be false. It takes for granted that baptism has come in the room of circumcision, which I have shewn to be false. It takes for granted that baptism is a door to a church, which I have shewn to be false. It takes for granted that the Christian Church and the Jewish nation are the same, which is not only false, but absurd.

It is sometimes said that if the Jewish nation contained unconverted persons, so do our churches. I answer, the very constitution, the organization, of the Jewish nation, admitted unconverted persons. No qualification whatever of a moral character was required. The constitution of a Christian Church requires a credible profession of piety, although those who profess may deceive others, or be themselves deceived.

"But if children are not baptized, then the Jewish Church had greater privileges than the Christian." With as much reason may it be said, that the Jewish Church had greater privileges than the Christian, because slaves are not baptized when purchased, or because members are not admitted, like the Shechemites, that they may procure wives in the church.

In point of fact, with the glorious effulgence of Revelation all around us; with life and immortality assured to us and to our infants dying in infancy; with Christ saying Suffer little children to come unto me, and blessing them; with the full dispensation of the Holy Spirit; with Sabbath schools, and all the hallowed influences of the Gospel penetrating and imbuing the youthful heart from the very cradle; with all this, will any one compare the privileges of Christians with those enjoyed by a Jew?

This allegation proceeds entirely on the idea that circumcision was itself a great privilege: but was it so? We have seen that it did not secure any spiritual privilege; nor to the individual circumcised was it a guaranty even of temporal benefits. The females were entitled to these benefits as well as the males who were circumcised. Ishmael, slaves, the Shechemites, had no promise of a part of Canaan; yet they were circumcised. God, as a Sovereign, and for wise reasons, commanded this mark to be put upon a carnal people; but it was a painful yoke. In Acts xv. it is called "a yoke," a "burden." It was no loss, but a great privilege, to females, that they were exempt from it.

Perish the thought that the advantages of our children are inferior to those of a Jewish child! If they die in infancy, we can rejoice in the assurance of their salvation through him who "died for all." And if they live, God calls them to a nobler circumcision, a nobler seal. Under the Gospel " circumcision is that of the heart," (Rom. ii. 29;) and the seal of the Gospel is the witness of the Holy Spirit, " by whom we are sealed unto the day of redemption."

Let us not, for the sake of a palpable though deeply rooted error, confound the covenant of Redemption with the Jewish covenant. The Israelites were favored, but God " has provided some better thing for us." " For this is the covenant that I will make with the house of Israel after those days, saith the Lord: I will put my laws into their mind, and write them in their hearts: and I will be to them a God, and they shall be to me a people." (Heb. viii. 10.) Let us rejoice in the sublime, glorious, blessed covenant; and let us teach our children to believe in Jesus, that they may rejoice in it with us; that, so, both we and they may exclaim, in the language of filial adoration and gratitude:

> Great Father of mercies, thy goodness I own,
> And the covenant love of thy crucified Son;
> All hail to the Spirit, whose whisper divine
> Seals mercy, and pardon and righteousness mine.

The only remaining sophistry belonging to this part of the subject is taken from Paul's language as to the olive tree, in Rom. xi. I need not dwell, however, upon this argument, for in exposing the errors just indicated I have exposed this.

It assumes, (1) that circumcision secured spiritual blessings to the child; (2) that baptism is in the room of circumcision; (3) that baptism initiates into a church; and (4) that the Christian Church is a continuation of the Jewish nation. The fallacy of each of these assumptions is, I hope, by this time, quite transparent.

The fact is that the passage is perfectly plain, and nothing but an attempt to wrest it, in order to support infant baptism, has created any difficulty. The apostle says that many of the Jews had forfeited the advantages they posessed, and that the Gentile nations have been admitted to these advantages. Now, what are these advantages? Are they the promises of the Abrahamic covenant? Have the Gentiles the promise that Christ shall spring from them, and that they shall possess the land of Canaan? The meaning is obviously this: the Jews were the depositories of the truth; they were specially favored with the lights and blessings of revelation. They rejected this light; God, therefore, rejected them, and committed to the Gentiles the treasures which they had despised. The apostle himself puts this matter beyond dispute. "*What advantage then,*" (he says in this very Epistle,) "*hath the Jew, or what profit is there in circumcision? Much every way—chiefly because that unto them were committed the oracles of God.*" Rom. iii. 1. To have been entrusted with the Bible, was, then, the greatest advantage of the Jewish nation. This advantage God now extends to the Gentile nations.

Barnes (Com.)—" The meaning here is, that the Gentiles had been like the wild olive, unfruitful in holiness; that they had been uncultivated by the institutions of the true religion, and consequently had grown up in the wildness and sin of nature. The Jews had been like a cultivated olive long under the training and blessing of God."

I finish this chapter with a fine thought of Pascal's. "That the Messiah might be properly attested, it was requisite that there should be antecedent prophecies, kept by persons not liable to suspicion, of extraordinary diligence, fidelity, zeal, and general notoriety. For this purpose the Almighty chose a carnal people, to whom he entrusted the prophecies which foretold the Messiah as the deliverer and dispenser of those carnal blessings which they loved; this excited an ardent attachment to the writings of their prophets, which they held up to the view of the whole world, and assured all nations, that the predicted Messiah would come in the manner these writings specified. But, deceived by the appearance of the Messiah in abasement and poverty, they became his most virulent enemies. Thus that very people, who of all others can be least suspected of favoring us, have rendered the greatest service to our cause, and by their zeal for the law and the prophets, bear and preserve, with incorruptible fidelity, their own condemnation, and the evidences of our religion.". Pensees de Pascal, ch. viii.

CHAPTER VIII.

FORMERLY an argument for infant baptism used to be attempted from Jewish proselyte baptism, and I had designed here to expose this. I find, however, that it is now abandoned by all candid and learned men.

There is not an allusion to such a baptism in the Old or New Testament; not a word about it in the Apocryphal writings, nor in the works of Josephus or Philo, who, at the beginning of the Christian era, wrote on the subject of Jewish rites and customs. The first mention of this baptism is in the Mishna, written A. D. 220. Any one who will read Matt. xxi. 25, Mark, i. 1, 4, and John, i. 33, will see that baptism was a divine institution, new and perplexing to the Jews.

Dr. Jennings.—"But after all, it remains to be proved, not only that Christian baptism was instituted in the room of proselyte baptism, but that the Jews had any such baptism in our Saviour's time. The earliest accounts we have of it are in the Mishna and Gemara; the former compiled, as the Jews assert, by Rabbi Juda, in the second century; though learned men, in general, bring it several centuries lower; the latter not till the seventh century. There is not a word of it in Philo, nor yet in Josephus, though he gives an account of the proselyting of the Idumeans, by Hyrcanus."

Dr. Owen.—"The institution of the rite of baptism is nowhere mentioned in the Old Testament. There is no example of it in those ancient records; nor was it ever used in the admission of proselytes while the Jewish Church continued. No mention of it occurs in Philo, in Josephus, in Jesus the son of Sirach, nor in the Evangelical History. This Rabbinical opinion, therefore, owes

* Jew. Antiq. vol. i. p. 136.

its rise to the Tannera or Ante-Mishnical doctors, after the destruction of their city. The opinion of some learned men, therefore, about the transferring of a Jewish baptismal rite (which in reality did not then exist,) by the Lord Jesus, for the use of his disciples, is destitute of all probability."*

Dr. Lardner.—"As for the baptism of Jewish proselytes, I take it to be a mere fiction of the Rabbins, by whom we have suffered ourselves to be imposed upon."†

Prof. Neander, in his lectures, says,—"Since the elaborate work of Schneckenburger has appeared, no one will pretend that he can prove the existence of a proselyte baptism in the time of Christ."

Hase's Hutterus Redivivus, p. 341.—"A proselyte baptism, in the time of Christ, cannot be proved."

Bottiger, one of the greatest of the German antiquarians, affirms, that "the whole assertion (of a proselyte baptism before the time of John,) is perfectly destitute of proof."

CHAPTER IX.

I HAVE thus gone through both Testaments, and here I might stop, for I know no Bible but that which begins with Genesis, and ends with Revelations. Our brethren, however, have a forlorn hope; they try to find some

---

* Theologoum L. v. Dig. iv. † Lett. writ. Dodd. Lett. 89.

apology for infant baptism in early church history. Into that history, therefore, this chapter must take us. Bossuet, the most able of the Roman Catholic controversialists, says: "Experience has shewn that all the attempts of the reformed to confound the Anabaptists by the Scriptures, have been weak; and, therefore, they are at last obliged to allege to them the practice of the church."* And in the Roman Catholic "Manual of Controversy," we have the following question and answer:

Q. "But why should not the scripture alone be the rule of our faith, without having recourse to apostolical traditions?

A. Because infants' baptism, and several other necessary articles, are either not at all contained in scripture, or at least are not plain in scripture, without the help of tradition."

I enter at once into the matter, and begin with the FIRST CENTURY. We have inspired church history for the age of Christ and the apostles; and we have seen that infant baptism was unknown then. No writer in this century gives the slightest countenance to this surreptitious institution. My readers have often been told that it can be traced up to the time of the apostles. What will they say when they know that during the first hundred years there is not an allusion to such a practice? This is conceded by all who deal in fact, and not in reckless declamation.

Luther.—"It cannot be proved by the sacred scrip-

---

* Stennett to Russen.

ture that infant baptism was instituted by Christ, or begun by the first Christians after the apostles." *

M. de la Roque.—" The primitive church did not baptize infants; and the learned Grotius proves it, in his Annotations on the Gospel." †

Ludovicus Vives.—" No one, in former times, was admitted to the sacred baptistery, except he was of age, understood what the mystical water meant, desired to be washed in it, and expressed that desire more than once." ‡

Chambers.—" It appears that in the primitive times none were baptized but adults." §

Salmasius and Suicerus.—" In the first two centuries, no one was baptized, except, being instructed in the faith, and acquainted with the doctrine of Christ, he was able to profess himself a believer; because of those words, 'he that believeth, and is baptized.'" ‖

Curcellæus.—" The baptism of infants, in the first two centuries after Christ, was altogether unknown; but in the third and fourth was allowed by some few. In the fifth and following ages it was generally received. The custom of baptizing infants did not begin before the third age after Christ was born. In the former ages no trace of it appears, and it was introduced without the command of Christ." ¶

* In A. R.'s Vanity of Infant Baptism, part ii. p. 8.
† In Stennett's Answer to Russen, p. 188.
‡ Annotat. in Aug. de Civ. Dei. L. i. c. xxxvii.
§ Cyclopædia, Art. Baptism.
‖ Epist. ad. Justum Pacium. Thesaur. Eccles. sub. voce. Sunaxis, Tom. ii. p. 1136.
¶ Institut. Relig. Christ. L. i. c. xii.· Dissert. Secund. de Pecc. Orig. § 56.

Neander.—"It cannot possibly be proved that infant baptism was practised in the apostolic age. Its late introduction, the opposition it met with still in the second century, rather speak against an apostolical origin."*

Prof. Hahn's Theology, p. 557.—"Neither in the Scriptures, nor during the first hundred and fifty years, is a sure example of infant baptism to be found; and we must concede that the numerous opposers of it cannot be contradicted on gospel ground." Few men stand so high in public estimation, for piety, sense, and learning, as Prof. Hahn, of Breslau.

Myers, in his Commentary on Acts, xvi. 15.—"Baptism without faith never appears (in the Scripture,) and is contrary to Matt. xxxviii. 19 (the Commission.) The early and continued opposition to infant baptism would have been inexplicable if it had been an undoubted apostolical institution."†

Menzell.—"One of these last (abuses) was infant baptism, a departure from the original form of the sacrament, which had existed for centuries in the church, (for which, indeed, very pertinent reasons can be offered,) but it is nevertheless, a departure."‡

Second Century.—Is there evidence that infant baptism was known in this century? If known at all, it was only at the close of this century; but there is no

---

*Apost. Age, v. 1, p. 140.

† Myers' Critical Commentary on the New Testament. Gottingen, 1835, v. iii. p. 215.

‡ K. H. Menzell's Modern History of the Germans and the Reformation. Breslau, 1826, v. 1. p. 123.

proof of its introduction even then. The first writer of this century is Justin Martyr. Semler makes this concession: "From Justin Martyr's description of baptism, (second Apol. p. 93,) we learn that it was administered only to adults. He says, 'We were (corporeally) born without our will (*kat anagkén;*) but in baptism we are to have choice, knowledge, &c. This we learned from the apostles.' "*

Justin also gives us the account of baptism in his day, which shews that infants were not baptized, since it is a full exposition to the Emperor of all pertaining to the rite.

Justin Martyr.—"I will now declare unto you also after what manner we, being made new by Christ, have dedicated ourselves to God, lest, if I should leave out that, I might seem to deal unfairly in some part of my apology. They who are persuaded and do believe that those things which are taught by us are true, and do promise to live according to them, are directed first to pray, and ask of God, with fasting, the forgiveness of their former sins; and we also pray and fast together with them. Then we bring them to some place where there is water, and they are regenerated by the same way of regeneration by which we were regenerated; for they are washed in water in the name of God, the Father and Lord of all things, and of our Saviour Jesus Christ, and of the Holy Spirit."†

This passage expressly declares that the persons bap-

* Baumgarten's Rel. Controversies, v. 2, p. 64.
† Justini Apolog. Prim. ad Anton. Pi. 61.

tized were "persuaded and believed;" yet Dr. Peters foists infants into it. He asserts that Justin Martyr says, "Infants are washed with water in the name of the Father and Son and Spirit."*

The only other passage from Justin is this: "Several persons among us of sixty or seventy years old, and of both sexes, who were converted to Christ in their childhood, do continue uncorrupted."

This passage makes against infant baptism. The word

---

* Mr. Carson has been thought severe, but who can witness such things and be calm! The Berkshire Association recommend the work of Dr. Peters as "original," "and a short method of settling this question." I hope such an original will find no copies, and that few will adopt such "short methods." This same writer also affirms that the Greek Church practises sprinkling!! These will do as samples of Dr. Peters's facts. In logic his only "original" exploit is that of "the Greek Plow." *Arotron* is the Greek word for a Plow. "The Greek Plow," says Dr. Peters, "Was a straight stick," the "Yankee Plow" is different; therefore *Arotron*, if used by us, would "have a new meaning." By this he designs to shew that, though Baptizo meant *immerse* among the Greeks, it may now mean *sprinkle!* What is the use of trying to reason with such a man? It is plain he needs not argument, but physic.

Whatever be its model, a plow is still a plow; but vary it as you will, sprinkling is not immersion. Dr. Peters's propositions ought to be put thus. *Arotron* is the Greek for Plow. The Greek Plow was a straight stick; the moderns have changed the plow into a crooked stick, "with its colter, &c." It is still, however, a plow, and *Arotron* applies to it. *Baptizo* is the Greek for immerse. Christian Baptism is immersion. But Pædobaptists have changed it into sprinkling. It is, therefore, no longer immersion, and the word baptism does not apply to it.

which I translate "converted," is, in Justin, *Ematheusate*, the very word used by Christ in the Commission, to describe the teaching or preaching which must precede baptism. It means literally "taught." Bloomfield translates it, as I do, "convert to the faith." Justin does not allude to baptism. I produce this passage, as I wish to give all that history furnishes on the subject. I do not know that any one has ever laid any stress on it, as favoring infant baptism. Doddridge says:* "This may only refer to their having been early instructed in the Christian religion."

The next writer of this century is Irenæus. I will give a literal translation of the only passage in his works where our brethren pretend to discover infant baptism.

Irenæus.—"Therefore, as he (Christ) was a master, he had also the age of a master. Not disdaining nor going in a way above human nature, nor breaking in his own person the law which he had made for mankind; but sanctifying every several age by the likeness that it has to himself; for he came to save all persons by himself,—all, I mean, *who by him are born again (renascuntur) unto God,*—infants, and little ones, and children, and youths, and elder persons: therefore, he went through the several ages; for infants being made an infant, sanctifying infants; to little ones he was made a little one, sanctifying that age; and also giving an example of godliness, justice and dutifulness; to youths he was a youth, &c." †

Now no man, not seeking for something which never

* Misc. Works, Lect. civ. p. 494. † Iren. adv. Hæres. lib. ii. c. 39.

entered Irenæus's mind, could find any difficulty in this passage. It merely affirms that, in order to infuse the benefits of his atonement into every age, Christ passed through all ages. Our brethren, however contend that infant baptism is here. It is with astonishment and grief that I find one writer even mistranslating the passage, and inserting baptism into it. Mr. Slicer affirms that "Irenæus, who wrote within sixty-seven years of the apostolic times, says, 'Christ came to save all persons by himself, all, I mean, who by him are *baptized* (Mr. Slicer italicises the word baptized) unto God, infants, and little ones, and children, and youths!!!'"* Irenæus wrote A. D. 178, and the word baptize is not in the passage.

The whole plea founded on the above quotation is this: Baptismal regeneration had at this time begun to be received as a tenet, and when Irenæus uses the words "born again," (*renascuntur,*) he may mean baptized. This is the argument; but it is easily refuted. By the writers of this date the word *regeneration*, when used alone, refers to a spiritual change. When applied to baptism they combine other words, clearly showing their meaning. An example of this we have already given in our quotation from Justin Martyr, (see ante p. 189,) where the candidates are said to be regenerated by water. In the same treatise, Justin distinguishes between baptism and regeneration. Speaking of the Supper, he says, "Of which it is not lawful for any to partake, but such as believe the things we teach, and are

* Slicer on Baptism, p. 78.

baptized for the remission of their sins, and regeneration, &c." * In his dialogue with Trypho, he says, "Christ is become the head of another people, who are regenerated by him by water, faith, and the tree, &c."† Here regeneration is said to be by water, faith, and the cross. But is faith regeneration? Is the cross regeneration? Dr. Doddridge gives up this pretended argument from Irenæus. He says: "We have only a Latin translation of this work; and some critics have supposed this passage spurious; or, allowing it to be genuine, it will not be granted that to be regenerate always, in his writings, signifies baptized."‡

Prof. Sears has settled forever this matter by an elaborate investigation of the works of Irenæus.§ He gives abundant citations from this writer to prove that he never uses the words "born again" in the sense here pretended. Indeed, the passage itself shows that the words do not refer to baptism, for what nonsense to talk of persons being "baptized by Christ unto God." The meaning clearly is, born again, or converted unto God. The conclusions established by Dr. Sears, or rather by Irenæus himself, whom he brings forward, are these:—

1. The phrase "regenerated through Christ unto God," if it mean the general "recovery of man through Christ's incarnation and redemption," has numerous

---
* Just. Apol. p. 97.   † P. 367.
‡ Dodd. Miscel. Works, p. 493.
§ See Christ. Rev. June, 1838.

parallels in the writings of Irenæus; if it mean "baptized through Christ unto God," it has no parallel—absolutely none.

2. The phrase "baptism through Christ unto God," is an incongruous idea, nowhere to be found in the Scriptures, in the writings of Irenæus, or in any other father or writer, ancient or modern.

3. "Regeneration," standing alone, without any such words as "baptism," or "bath," prefixed, and governing it in the genitive, never means baptism in Irenæus.

4. That Christ sanctified infants, by becoming an infant himself, has several parellels in Irenæus. "He became an infant to aid our weak apprehension." "He became an infant with us on this account." "He went into Egypt, sanctifying the infants that were there." It would be absurd to suppose that the infant Jesus baptized the Egyptian infants.

5. That by passing through the several stages of human life, from infancy to old age, he sanctified human nature in these various ages, by his own incarnation and example, is an idea often repeated by Irenæus, and by modern writers, too, as Sartorius. But if this be limited to baptism, or to the baptized, it will contradict what he elsewhere says.

6. The general character of his redemption and regeneration, as expressed in this passage, according to our interpretation, is a favorite idea with our author; a similar sentiment in regard to baptism is not to be found in his writings.

7. The connection of the latter part of the sentence

INFANT BAPTISM. 195

with the former, as explaining or amplifying the idea, is weakened if not destroyed by the other interpretation.

I add the following concessions from authors whose reputation for profound ecclesiastical learning is in all the world.

Baumgarten Crusius, p. 1209.—"The celebrated passage in Irenæus is not to be applied to infant baptism; for the phrase '*Renasci per eum* (that is, *Christum*,) *in Deum*,' evidently means the participation of all his divine and holy nature, in which he became a substitute for all."

Winer (in his lectures.)—"Tertullian is the first that mentions it (infant baptism.) Irenæus does not mention it, as has been supposed."

Rossler (in his Library of the Christian Fathers, v. i. p. 11.) "All the arguments put together do not prove that '*Renasci in Deum*' (in this passage of Irenæus) means to be baptized."

Von Coln, vol. i. p. 469.—"All the earlier traces of infant baptism are very uncertain. Tertullian is the first who mentions it, and he censures it."

Suicer (Thesaurus Ecclesiasticus, a work containing a digest of the voluminous theological writings of the Greek Fathers.)—"In the first two centuries no one received baptism, unless (being instructed in the faith, and imbued with the doctrine of Christ,) he could testify that he was a believer, on account of these words: 'He that believeth and is baptized.' Therefore, to believe preceded. Thence arose in the church the order of catechumens. It was also then the constant custom that the eucharist should be given to those catechumens immediately after baptism. Afterwards the opinion prevailed, that no one could be saved unless he had been baptized. But because formerly the eucharist was given to adult catechumens as soon as they had been bathed in sacred baptism, this also was appointed to be done in the case of infants, after Pædobaptism was introduced."* This is the declaration of such a scholar as Suicer, after twenty years' indefatigable researches among the writings of the early Christian fathers.

In the Bibliotheca Sacra and Theological Review, vol. vi., there is a most learned examination of this passage. To ascertain its meaning, the author, Dr. Chase, read and re-read every line of all the extant works of Irenæus. After a careful investigation he thus sums up his convictions (pp. 646, 656.) "According to Irenæus, Christ, in becoming incarnate, and thus assuming his mediatorial work, brought the human family into a new relation, under himself, and placed them in a condition in which they can be saved. In this sense, he is the Saviour of all. He restored them, or summed them up anew, in himself. He became, so to speak, a second Adam, the regenerator of mankind. Through him they are regenerated unto God; *per eum renascuntur in Deum.*

" The thought occurs frequently, and it is variously modified by the various connections in which it is introduced.

" In the passage which has often been brought forward

Tom. ii. p. 1131, Art. Sunazis. iv.

as recognizing the baptism of infants, Irenæus is maintaining that Christ appeared as he really was, and passed through the various stages of human life, sanctifying, it is added, sanctifying every age by the likeness that it had to himself; *for he came to save all by himself; all, I say, since by him they are regenerated unto God*—infants and little ones, and children, and youths, and elder persons. Therefore he came through the several ages, and for infants was made an infant sanctifying infants; among little ones, a little one, sanctifying those of that age—and at the same time, being to them an example of piety, uprightness and obedience; among the youth, a youth, becoming an example to the youths, and sanctifying them to the Lord; thus also an elderly person, among elderly persons, that he might be a perfect master among all, not only in respect to the presentation of truth, but also in respect to age, sanctifying at the same time also the elderly persons, and becoming to them an example. Then, too, he passed through even unto death, that he might be the first born from the dead, himself holding the primacy in all things, the prince of life, superior to all, and preceding all. B. ii. c. 22, § 4.

"What Irenæus thought of baptism must be gathered from the passages in which he is speaking of the subject. But that he is speaking of it in this passage, there is no sufficient evidence. For a mere resemblance in one or two words to certain terms sometimes used in connection with baptism, falls very far short of proving the point assumed. The context is against it, for the context directs our attention to *Christ*, and what he himself personally came to do for the human family. It is by *Him*, and not by baptism, that they are here said to be renewed, born anew, or regenerated. And parallel passages are against it, for they abundantly confirm the sense which I have given, as being the true sense of the passage before us."

We come, now, to the celebrated Tertullian, who wrote at the close of the second century. He alludes to the baptism of "little ones," but not to that of infants; and he opposes the baptism of "little ones." Here is what Tertullian says: "That baptism ought not to be administered rashly, the administrators of it know. 'Give to him that asketh, every one hath a right;' as if it were a matter of alms. Yea, rather say, Give not that which is holy unto dogs, cast not your pearls before swine, lay hands suddenly on no man, be not a partaker of other men's sins. If Philip baptized the Eunuch on the spot, let us recollect it was done under the immediate direction of the Lord. The Spirit commanded Philip to go that way; the Enunch was not idle when he found him, nor did he immediately desire to be baptized; but having been at the temple to worship God, he was attending to the Holy Scriptures. There was a propriety in what he was about, when God sent his apostle to him; the Spirit gave Philip a second order to join himself to the chariot. The Eunuch was a believer of Scripture; the instruction given by Philip was seasonable; the one preached, and the other perceived the Lord Jesus, and believed on him; water was at hand, and the apostle having finished the affair was caught away. But Paul, you say, was baptized instantly. True: because Judas, in whose house he was, instantly knew he was a vessel of mercy. The condescension of God may confer his favors as he pleases; but our wishes may mislead ourselves and others. It is therefore most expedient to defer baptism and to regulate the administration of it according to the condition, the disposition, and the age of the person to be baptized: and especially in the case of little ones. What necessity is there to expose sponsors to danger? Death may incapacitate them for fulfilling their engagements; or bad disposition may defeat all their endeavors. Indeed, the Lord saith, 'Forbid them not to come unto me;' and let them come while they are growing up, let them come and learn, and let them be instructed when they come, and when they understand Christianity let them profess themselves Christians. Why should that innocent age hasten to the remission of sins? People act more cautiously in secular affairs; they do not commit the care of divine things to such as are not entrusted with temporal things. *They just know how to ask for salvation, that you may seem to give to him that asketh.*"*

Now as to this passage two remarks must at once suggest themselves to every candid reader. First, it does not refer to babes. The "little ones" here spoken of "knew how to ask for salvation;" and of them Tertullian says, "Let them come, and let them be instructed when they come, and when they understand Christianity let them profess themselves Christians."

* Robinson's History of Baptism, pp. 174–176.

They were, therefore, old enough to be instructed, and he requires this before baptism. The mention of sponsors does not prove anything as to the age of the children; for sponsors were employed in the cases of adults as well as infants. Mosheim, v. i. p.—" Adult persons were prepared for baptism by abstinence, prayer, and other pious exercises. It was to answer for them that sponsors or god-fathers were first instituted, though they were afterwards admitted also in the baptism of infants.

But, secondly, Tertullian condemns the baptism even of these children who were plainly not infants. This, of course, would have been impossible if infant baptism had then been regarded as an apostolical institution.

Neander (Church Hist. vol. i. part 2, p. 364.)—Towards the close of the second century, Tertullian appears as a zealous opposer of infant baptism;—a proof that it was not yet customary to regard this as an apostolic institution; for had it been so, he would hardly have ventured to oppose it so warmly."

In his Spirit of Tertullian, p. 207, Neander says:— "For these reasons, Tertullian declared against infant baptism, which at that time was certainly not a generally prevailing practice—was not yet regarded as an apostolic institution. On the contrary, as the assertions of Tertullian render in the highest degree probable, it had just begun to spread, and was, therefore, regarded by many as an innovation."

Dr. Barlow (Bishop of Lincoln, in his letter to Mr. Tombs.)—" I believe and know that there is neither precept nor example in Scripture for Pædobaptism, nor any just evidence for it for about two hundred years after Christ. Sure I am, that in the primitive times they were catechumeni, then illuminati, or baptizati. The truth is, I do believe Pædobaptism, how or by whom I know not, came into the world in the second century, and in the third or fourth began to be practised, though not generally."

Curcellæus.—Pædobaptism was not known in the world the two first ages after Christ. In the third and fourth it was approved of by a few. At length, in the fifth and following ages, it began to obtain in divers places. And, therefore, we observe this rite indeed as an ancient custom, but not as an apostolical tradition. The custom of baptizing infants did not begin before the third age after Christ; and there appears not the least footstep of it in the two first centuries."*

The celebrated German critic, Bretschneider, Theol. (1838) vol. i. p. 469.—"All the earlier traces of infant baptism are very doubtful; on the contrary, Tertullian is the first who refers to it, and he censures it."

Winer (Manuscript Lectures.) — "Originally only adults were baptized; but at the end of the second century, in Africa, and in the third century, generally, infant baptism was introduced; and in the fourth century, it was theologically maintained by Augustine."

Rheinwald, p. 313.—"The first traces of infant baptism are found in the Western Church, after the middle

* Crosby's Hist. pref. p. 66.

of the second century, and it was the subject of controversy in Pro-consular Africa towards the end of this century. Though its necessity was asserted in Africa and Egypt in the beginning of the third century, it was, even to the end of the fourth century, by no means universally observed—least of all in the Eastern Church. Notwithstanding the recommendation of it by the fathers, it never became a general ecclesiastical institution, till the age of Augustine."

THIRD CENTURY.—In this century manifold corruptions were introduced into the Christian system. Infant baptism entered with other corruptions. It was, however, so plain an innovation that we find those who practised it perplexed with difficulties. The letter of Fidus, a country bishop, (A. D. 248,) to Cyprian, is a striking proof of this. Fidus writes to know "if an infant may be baptized before the eighth day?" A question which could never have arisen, had not infant baptism been then a novel and unsettled thing.*

Another distinguished writer of this century, Origen, makes this remark: "Having occasion given in this place, I will mention a thing which causes frequent inquiries among the brethren. Infants are baptized for the forgiveness of sins. Of what sins? or when have they sinned? or how can any reason of the laver in their case hold good, but according to the sense that we mentioned even now, viz: 'None is free from pollution, though his life be but the length of one day upon the

---

* Cyp. (Epis. lxiv.) ad Fidum.

earth?' and it is for that reason, because by the sacrament of baptism the pollution of our birth is taken away, that infants are baptized."* How plain from this passage that infant baptism was a new thing even at this late day, and its advocates puzzled by it.

Another passage is often cited by our opponents, from Origen. It is this: "For this also it was that the church had from the apostles, a tradition to give baptism even to infants; for they to whom divine mysteries were committed knew that there is in all persons the natural pollution of sin, which must be done away by water and the Spirit; by reason of which the body itself is also called the body of sin."†

Dr. Gale pronounces this passage spurious. Dr. Doddridge says of Origen's writings: "They are chiefly to be found in those translations of his Greek works which were done by Ruffinus and Jerome, who made some very bold alterations according to their own judgment and taste; but this is not applicable to all the passages brought from him."‡

I, for my part, do not think it worth while to examine the genuineness of the passage. I make but two observations. First, admitting the words to be Origen's, even he gives up all scripture authority, and only pretends that there was a tradition, and rests infant baptism on the virtue of water to take away sin. Do our

---

* Origen, Homil. in Luc. 14.
† Comment. in Epist. ad. Romanos, lib. v.
‡ Dodd. Miscel. Works, p. 944.

bethren concur in all this? If so, they yield the question. Then, as for his assertion about a tradition, Neander says: "His words, in that age, cannot have much weight: for whatever was regarded as important was alleged to be from the apostles. Besides, many walls of partition intervened between this age, and that of the apostles, to intercept the view."*

Let it be remembered, too, that those fathers who defend infant baptism in this century, defend also infant communion. Dr. Doddridge says: "Cyprian is allowed by all to speak expressly of infant baptism as generally used in the church; but it is justly answered, that he speaks as expressly of infant communion in the eucharist; and consequently that the divine original of the latter may as well be argued from him, as that of the former; yet almost all Pædobaptists allow that to be an innovation."†

FOURTH CENTURY.—Christianity was now thoroughly corrupt. Taylor, in his admirable work on Ancient Christianity, thus writes: There is no degradation of the intellect, no bondage of the moral sentiments, no fatal substitution of forms for realities; there is no ineffable drivelling belonging to the middle age monkery that may not be matched to the full in the monkery of the bright times of Chrysostom, Ambrose, and Augustine. I here put the question aloud to any opponent, What is it that you precisely mean by the corruptions of popery

---

* Church History, vol. i. part ii. p. 367.
† Dodd. Miscel. Works, p. 494.

in respect to the monastic system? or, in other words, Can you make it appear, to the satisfaction of thinking men, that this same system had become more frivolous, and, therefore, in a religious sense, more pernicious, in the twelfth century, than it was at the opening of the fourth?"*

Yet even in this century, we find such a man as Gregory Nazianzen, the metropolitan of all Greece, the most illustrious man of his day, treating infant baptism as an innovation, and recommending that it be administered only in cases where death is imminent. In his fortieth oration he thus speaks: "But, say some, what is your opinion of infants, who are not capable of judging either of the grace of baptism, or of the damage sustained by the want of it; shall we baptize them too? By all means, if there be any apparent danger. For it were better they were sanctified without their knowing it, than that they should die without being sealed or initiated. As for others, I give my opinion, that when they are three years of age, or thereabouts, (for then they are able to hear and answer some of the mystical words, and, although they do not fully understand, they may receive impressions,) they may be sanctified, both soul and body, by the great mystery of initiation."†

Augustine flourished in the latter part of the fourth and beginning of the fifth centuries. He was a violent advocate of infant baptism. He speaks of opposition

---

* Ancient Christianity, p. 149.
† Robinson's History of Baptism, p. 249.

to it in his day, and is bitter against the Donatists, a party who still rejected this error.

Even in the FIFTH CENTURY we find Boniface, Bishop of Rome, treating infant baptism as a thing scarcely to be defended. He thus writes to Augustine: "Suppose I set before you an infant, and ask you whether, when he grows up, he will be a chaste man or a thief? Your answer, doubtless, will be, I cannot tell. And whether he, in that infant age, have any good or evil thoughts? You will say, I know not. Since you, therefore, dare not say anything, either concerning his future behaviour or his present thoughts, what is the meaning, that when they are brought to baptism, their parents, or sponsors for them, make answer and say, to the inquiry, 'Does he believe in God?' they answer, 'He does believe!' . . . I entreat you to give me a short answer to these questions, in such a manner as that you *do not urge to me the prescription or the customariness of the thing, but give me the reason of the thing.*"

CHAPTER X.

WITH regard to some of the corruptions of Christianity, we cannot help wondering how they could ever have been palmed upon men; but, as to infant baptism, we feel no surprise. At a very early period baptism was regarded as washing away guilt, and as absolutely necessary to save from Adam's sin. This creed once received, infant baptism directly secured its place in the parental feeling, where, in fact, it now finds its only respectable apology.

In concluding this part of my work, let me entreat my readers to discard a practice which is so palpable a departure from the law of Christ. We are often told that infant baptism can do no harm; this, however, is a great mistake. We cannot alter any part of the gospel system without doing harm. Many of our Pædobaptist brethren virtually abandon this error; and even ministers, while they maintain that it is a solemn command of Christ, yet do not require it of their members. Where, indeed, is the pastor who would venture at this day to enforce infant baptism in his church?

But it is not enough that we abstain from this unchristian practice. We ought to seek its abrogation. I know that in many of the most devoted families, where this error has been transmitted through a long line of honored ancestors, its condemnation by one of the members would be regarded as heinous apostacy. And I know, too, it requires no little heroism to renounce and wrestle with the sanctities of old opinions and hereditary prejudices. If we love Christ, however, we ought steadfastly to resist infant baptism. Why? Listen, I am going to tell you in so many words.

And, first, *infant baptism makes void the commandment of God by a human tradition.* In the Old Testament one of the complaints of God against Israel is, that they "changed his ordinance." In the New Testament Jesus charges the Pharisees with the same sin. Children were required by God to support their parents when poor. The Pharisees superseded this precept, allowing the child to swear by the Corban. "Full well," said the Saviour, "ye reject the commandment of God, that ye may keep your own tradition." It is just thus with infant baptism. Jesus commands men to believe and be baptized. Infant baptism makes void this command by a tradition; and if it prevailed universally, the command of Christ, that is, the Commission, would be entirely abolished, and another institution substituted for Christian baptism.

Secondly. *Infant baptism has introduced and perpetuated among Christians the most glaring and mischievous confusion and inconsistency as to Churches and Church membership.*

As we have before remarked,* the word *Church*, when religiously used, has only two meanings in the New Testament. It means either the whole company of the converted, or a particular society. Now it will not be pretended that, either by birth or baptism, an infant is made a member of the Church in the first sense. It must, therefore, be a member of some particular visible society. But is this true? Take any one of the Pædobaptist Churches in this city, and tell me, does that church regard all the infants baptized there as really members? Ministers call them members; but

---

* See this more fully considered in Part III.

that they are not considered as members is manifest. For they are not reported among the members; they are not admitted to any of the privileges of members; they are never dealt with when they grow up, no matter how they behave; in fact, it would be a matter of amazement and derision to these persons if they should be summoned before the church as members. Lastly, when, afterwards, they profess to be converted, this very minister and church declare that *they have joined the Church!* they are then taken in on probation, or to full fellowship! In all this, what confusion and contradiction.

A third evil of infant baptism. *It destroys entirely the significancy of baptism.* Properly administered, baptism is a most speaking ordinance. It is beautifully emblematical of Christ's death and resurrection, and of our own dying unto sin and rising to a new life. If infant baptism prevailed, how would all this, and the benefit of all this, be lost!

A fourth reason why infant baptism ought to cease. *It reflects injuriously upon God, and tarnishes the glory of the atonement.* It originated in the frightful dogma of infant damnation; and still connives at and fosters that abominable heresy. It nourishes, also, that other heresy to which men are so prone, which detracts from the fullness and freeness of the atonement; for it insinuates that we must do something, or our children cannot be saved.

The system of infant baptism, if carried out, would break down the distinction between the Church and the world. Here is a fifth objection to it. Christ's "kingdom is not of this world;" its subjects are spiritual, and spiritually born. But if infants are members of this kingdom, then this distinction ceases. It is, in fact, only by practically denying their own doctrine, and adopting that of the Baptists, that our brethren still preserve the line of separation between the Church and the world.

Infant baptism subverts the great principle of individual responsibility. This is my sixth objection. In obedience or disobedience to God every one must "give account of himself." Obedience by a human substitute is absurd. Once, indeed, the universe witnessed an amazing phenomenon—a Divine Being voluntarily placing Himself "under the Law" and satisfying its claims for His people. But to obey by a human proxy, is plainly impossible. Jesus commands all men to *be baptized*, just as he enjoins repentance. Pædobaptists would scout the idea that a parent can repent for the child, yet they hold that, by a parental act, the child can obey the command to be baptized.

I add a seventh evil of infant baptism. *It perpetuates unhappy and pernicious divisions among Christians.* Instead of pouring their united strength upon the territories of darkness and sin, what are Christians doing? They are frustrating the Gospel by dissensions among themselves. We see the heritage of Jesus Christ broken up into fragments, all engaged in nothing with more hearty goodwill than secretly hating each other. In apostolic days it was *Christ*, now it is *Church*. "Lo here is the Church!" and "Lo there!" resound on every side. Each family has its creed, its system, which, like any other heir-loom, lineally descends and is received upon credit. The religion of multitudes is not loyalty to Christ, nor to truth, but to family and to church. The prejudices of birth and education gather strength with our years, and decide everything. They decide our faith. They decide our preacher; in whom the first virtue we require is, that he be as prejudiced as ourselves; that he carefully exclude light upon certain unpleasant topics, and be the champion, not of the Bible, but of the opinions we have inherited. Lastly, these prejudices, engrafted with so much pains in childhood, decide our party. The first religious impulse fixes us (without reflection, without a moment's examination of subjects on which salvation is suspended, and as to which the very diversity of sentiment warns us to be careful;) the first religious impulse fixes us in society where every thing conspires to enslave us irreclaimably; where the prejudices of a sect are added to the prejudices of family; and where party-spirit, that bane of truth, that curse and pest of Christianity, seals up the mind, and envenoms the heart, and bows down the whole man under a bigotry, blind, fierce, intolerant, vindictive, debasing and incurable.

These melancholy truths no one deplores more than I, but it is vain to deny them. Oh! when, when shall this mournful spectacle cease? When shall the last prayer of Christ be fulfilled? When shall we "all be one?" What heart but longs for that hour,

> When every sect shall fall,
> And Christ, the common Lord, be Lord of all?

Let the error I have been combating be abandoned, and a long advance will have been made towards truth and love and harmony. All controversy about baptism would soon disappear, if our children were allowed to grow up and decide for themselves from God's word. Nor would this be all. Infant baptism renounced, Protestants could no longer be blind to other errors, which are either necessary to its defense or grow out of it, and which foster jealousies, heart-burnings, and dissensions.

The last mischievous consequence of this practice is, *the injury it does to our children.* God forbid that I should represent an infant's eternal destiny as at all affected by a parent's sprinkling a few drops of water upon it. But if this child grows up, Christ requires it to be baptized. Infant baptism forestalls all inquiry as to this duty. It furnishes an opiate to the conscience, which prevents examination, and thus causes our children to live and die unbaptized. What parent will thus prejudice the cause of truth in the mind of his offspring? What father or mother is willing to consecrate error in the heart of a child, and thus to render it almost certain that the child will die in disobedience? Our brethren constantly appeal to the feelings of parents in behalf of infant baptism; to these tender feelings I would, as a parent, address myself, and plead against this error in the name of our children, as well as on behalf of God.

I have done. If this essay has convinced any of my readers, I now affectionately but solemnly conjure them to "arise and be baptized, and wash away their sins, calling on the name of the Lord." (Acts, xxii. 16.) Recollect, that whatever differences of sentiment exist as to baptism, there can be no difference as to the doom of him who sees a command but will not obey it. God can no more save such a man, than he can call light, darkness, or truth, error. Perhaps you were baptized in infancy; well, your parents did what they esteemed their duty. But baptism is not a command to *your parent*, it is a command *to you;* and their act can be no substitute for your obedience. The parents of Jesus circumcised him, yet he was afterwards baptized. Make him your example. Hear his voice which now cries to you, "If any man will come after me, let him deny himself, and take up his cross and follow me." I am supposing you were baptized (*immersed*) in infancy. If, however, it was only sprinkling, or pouring, recollect that, even had you then been a proper subject, still are you unbaptized.

What shall I say to those who have honored these pages with a candid perusal, and are yet unconvinced? What? Why, only this: Let us still love each other "with pure hearts fervently." Far be it from me, either to interfere with your right of private judgment, or to question your sincerity. If you have laid aside every prejudice, and with a perfect willingness and sincere desire to know the truth, have investigated this subject, and still differ from me, who am I, that I should presumptuously judge my brother? No; I will love my brother. I will still pray that my brother may be guided into the truth. For him, as for myself, I will still supplicate the aids of the Holy Spirit, that we may spend our days in peace and holiness, and be prepared for the solemn hour when we must stand before God; the hour when, alone with his conscience and his crimes, each shall find himself at the foot of the dread tribunal, there to have the secrets of our hearts scrutinized by that Eye, compared with whose glances the gaze of a gathered universe would only be "like the stupid stare of an idiot."

PART THIRD.

THE TERMS OF COMMUNION;

OR THE

RELATION OF BAPTISM TO THE SUPPER.

Acts, xxviii. 22. "But we desire to hear of thee what thou thinkest; for as concerning this sect, we know that every where it is spoken against."

Of whom is this said? What pernicious and pestilent sect was this, which thus every where attracted reproach and obloquy? The people here mentioned were the first Christians; and, whatever becomes of the famous dispute about apostolical succession to the "invisible gift," it will be conceded on all hands, I suppose, that upon the Baptist churches has descended, in unmitigated entail, the not very enviable distinction noticed in this passage.

In all ages the Baptists have opposed persecution; have asserted the glorious right of liberty of conscience for every man; and have sought only to persuade men to cast off spiritual tyranny, whether of state or creed, or church, or priest, and to obey the laws of Jesus. Yet in all ages they have been, and they still are, "every where spoken against." By too many professed Christians, indeed, they have been treated with a wantonness of invective which the Bible forbids even in the case of the devil himself. Jude tells us that "Michael, the archangel, when contending with the devil, he disputed about the body of Moses, durst not bring against him *a railing accusation.*" But, when disputing about baptism, how many railing accusations have not been brought against us, in and out of the pulpit, by those we love.

Now, may heaven forbid that we should ever return railing for railing; but, contrariwise, blessing. When the Holy Spirit visibly decended, it was not in the form of a falcon, but a dove; and with the spirit of peace and love we pray that we and our brethren may ever be filled.

Truth, however, is dearer to us than even peace and love. Indeed, there can be neither real peace nor love without truth. "The wisdom that cometh from on high is first *pure*, then peaceable." "Charity rejoiceth not in error, but rejoiceth in the truth." Politics is the science of compromises; but truth, above all, religious truth, can know no compromise with falsehood.

As to some of the scoffs from time to time shed upon us as a denomination, we are not careful to answer them. We will live them down. Our opponents themselves are beginning to do us tardy justice, as they comprehend our views. Soon even anonymous malice will cease to confound our doctrines with the turbulence of a few German fanatics in the age of Luther. The term **Anabaptists** will soon be remembered by our brethren only with regret; and the echoes which have come down to us from other days, and which are now heard but faintly, will, of themselves, ere long die away.

Other charges against us spring from such entire ignorance of facts, that they will be heard with surprise by all, of every name, who have studied history. For example, what shall we say of the assertion so often put forth, that the Baptists are a new sect? Have I not proved that the first churches were Baptist churches? If, after the death of the apostles, error had inundated the churches, and if this error had been perpetuated till to-day, what would be our duty? Ought we to continue in error? Would we not be bound to make the New Testament our rule, and to return to the primitive order and purity of the gospel?

But the singularity of this indictment is, that it recoils inevitably upon our brethren themselves. Again, and again, we sincerely love these brethren, though we differ from them. The origin of their churches is, however, confessedly of recent date; while, as to ours, no memory of man, no record of history, runneth back to a time later than the time of the apostles, when they were not. This fact is incontestable, "our enemies themselves being judges," as the subjoined quotations abundantly testify.

The first authority is Cardinal Hosius, at the Council of Trent, A. D. 1542. He said, "If the truth of religion were to be judged by the readiness and cheerfulness which a man of any sect shews in suffering, then the opinion and persuasion of no sect can be truer or surer than that of the Anabaptists; since there have been none, for these twelve hundred years past, that have been more grievously punished, or that have more cheerfully and steadfastly undergone, and even offered themselves to the most cruel sorts of punishment, than these people." "The Anabaptists are a pernicious sect, of which kind the Waldensians seem also to have been. Nor is this heresy a modern thing, for it existed in the time of Augustine."*

My next authority is Mosheim. He says, "The true origin of that sect which acquired the denomination of Anabaptists, by their administering anew the rite of baptism to those who came over to their communion, and derived that of Mennonites, from the famous man to whom they owe the greatest part of their present felicity, is hid in the remotest depths of antiquity, and is, of consequence, extremely difficult to be ascertained."†

I only add the following testimony from a volume entitled "*The History of the Origin of the Dutch Baptists,*" published, 1819, by Dr. Upeig, Theological Professor at Groningen, and the Rev. Mr. Dermont, Chaplain to the King of the Netherlands. "The Baptists may be considered as the only Christian community which has stood since the days of the apostles, and as a Christian society which has preserved pure, the doctrines of

---

* Rees' reply to Walker, p. 220; and apud Schyn Hist. Mennonit, p. 135.

† Eccles. Hist. v. iv. p. 439.

the Gospel, through all ages. The perfectly correct external and internal economy of the Baptist denomination tends to confirm the truth, disputed by the Romish church, that the Reformation brought about in the sixteenth century, was in the highest degree necessary; and at the same time goes to refute the erroneous notions of the Catholics that their communion is the most ancient."

The only accusation against the Baptist churches, which, to my mind, has any semblance of justice, is that of illiberality in what is called Close Communion. I desire to examine this charge. I, myself, was once strongly opposed to this practice; and verily thought, when I united with the Baptists, that "I ought to do many things against it, which also I did." Soon, however, I was made to feel, that a Christian is to obey, not his wishes and feelings, but truth and principle; and that truth and principle required me to conform to this custom. The reasons for this conclusion, which I arrived at most reluctantly and mutinously, I will lay before my reader, requesting of him a candid hearing.

CHAPTER I.

Now, in order to enter aright into the matter, I begin with the remark, made in the second part of this essay, that the Greek word translated *Church* in our Bible, means simply an *Assembly*. As there stated, it is applied in the New Testament even to a tumultuous mob; and, in a religious sense, has two, and only two, meanings; designating either the spiritual body of all who are converted, or a particular society meeting in any place for religious purposes.

Some there are, I am aware, who deny the existence of that body which I have called the spiritual church. I submit, however, to these bretheren, that the Scriptures do use the word church with this signification. There are passages which certainly do not refer to any but the spiritual body. For example, Eph. i. 22, 23, "And hath put all things under his feet, and given him to be the head over all things to the church, which is his body, the fulness of Him that filleth all in all." So, Coloss. i. 18, "And he is the head of the body the church."

But if these brethern err, their error is of little consequence compared with that of another party whom I shall presently mention, who seek to erect a third church a *tertium quid*, unknown to the Bible, and furnishing a refuge for the most pernicious corruptions.

The spiritual "body of Christ" is indeed a "glorious Church." This is the Catholic or Universal Church. To this belong none but the truly regenerate; they are the members of this society, knit together by a union not imaginary, but most sweet, and dear, and imperishable. Against this church the gates of hell shall never prevail. We rejoice in the hope that, in all the visible **churches** of different denominations, there **are those** who are united with us in this spiritual church. We delight to feel ourselves one with them; one in spirit, one in aim, one in 'a good hope through grace,' in short, one in Christ. The communion of this body, however, is not in material emblems, as bread and wine, it is spiritual; it is the fellowship of soul with soul; nor can walls, nor mountains, nor oceans, nor ages, separate those who are thus cemented. On the other hand, where this union does not exist, vainly do we speak of spiritual fellowship. People may worship in the same edifice, and sit side by side at the Lord's Table, but there is a world between them; in fact, they belong to two different worlds.

As to the other import of the term church, there is no difference of opinion among Christians. All agree that the word, when used in the Bible, is generally an appellation designating some particular society. We find, in fact, nothing in the Scriptures like the ecclesiastical organizations of which we now hear so much, as the Anglican Church, the Episcopal Church, the Presbyterian, Methodist, Baptist Church. When the · Holy Ghost alludes to the Christians in Judea, or Asia, or Macedonia, or Galatia, it is, not the Judean, or Asiatic, or Macedonian, or Galatian Church, but the churches in Judea, in Asia, in Macedonia, or Galatia. And this is constantly the phraseology of the New Testament, as the following, out of a multitude of passages, fully prove: "As I teach every where in *every church*." "Paul went through Syria confirming the *churches*." "The *churches* of Christ salute you." "So ordain I in *all the churches.*" "The care of all *the churches,*" &c. &c. As to these visible churches, and this import of the word, there is no dispute between any of our brethren and ourselves. It is also manifest, that these visible churches are not to be confounded with the Spiritual Church. None, indeed, ought to belong to these bodies, except those who are members of the spiritual body; but God alone can discern the wheat from the tares, and in the purest visible societies there will be those who have never been truly regenerated and born of God. Occasionally, as in 1 Cor. xii. 28, the term church is used collectively. In these cases it is evident that no new body is intended. The word there is generic—comprehending all the visible churches.

Besides these two churches the New Testament knows no other. But another has been fabricated, a *worldly church, a carnal body of Christ* (what words to be united!) and this anti-christian amalgamation is called "The Visible Church." Upon this figment Romanism rests, and from it all the semi-popery of Protestantism,—the corruption of Church and State, spiritual tyranny, ecclesiastical arrogance, and priestly usurpation,—all has sprung. That good men still cling to this heresy is greatly to be deplored. Until it be abandoned, Romanism cannot be successfully assailed. Nor do I believe that our brethren could fail to see the dangerous consequences of upholding so apochryphal an invention, were it not that this structure is needed as an asylum for infants. Are infants really regenerated by water, and made members of the spiritual church? This is Puseyism; it is a falsehood, exposed by a thousand living proofs to the contrary. Are infants made members of the visible churches in which they are baptized? This is an absurdity which these churches themselves practically repel. How then?—of what church is an infant a member? It is here that the figment before us is pressed into the service. It is only in a cloud of words about "the visible church," and an infinitely confused idea of some resemblance between the carnal nation of the Jews and this carnal church, that infant baptism finds a hiding place.

The following passage, from one of the ablest German writers, is full of instruction:—"When the unity of the church is spoken of in the New Testament, it is a moral unity which is intended. . . . But there gradually arose, after the second and third centuries, an entirely different conception of the unity of the church. It first originated among the Fathers in the West, in consequence of their transferring to Christianity certain incorrect Jewish ideas, which were disapproved by Jesus and his appostles, and which had the most injurious results. The unity of the church was placed, by them, in an entire external agreement as to those doctrines and forms which were handed down from the times of the apostles, through the churches founded by them; and in the external connection and fellowship of the particular societies founded upon this agreement. . . . through these principles, and the consequences derived from them, the hierarchy was gradually established; and intolerance, and the spirit of persecution and anathematizing, became very prevalent. The Papel hierarchy rests entirely upon these principles, and originated from them. The principal bishops now established a kind of college. or secret society; and this unity of the church was made dependent, first, upon many heads, then, upon one visible Head of the church. And whoever ventured to dissent from the doctrine or the ordinances of the principal bishops, who held together and governed their churches, was excluded from church-fellowship, and declared a heretic." Knapp's Theology, v. 2, pp. 484, 486.

The whole conception of this worldly establishment is anti-christian. According to the gospel, a visible church is a society of believers united for religious purposes. In the church polity of the Redeemer, a person was converted and baptized, and then "added to the church." In process of time this order was inverted. Infants were added to the church that they might be afterwards converted. Thus sprang up a worldly hierarchy, and thus crept in that most mischievous of all the errors of Rome, I mean the idea that the church is a sort of sacred enclosure in which, mechanically and by machinery, people are absolved from sin and saved. "In the beginning of the gospel," says D'Aubigne, "whosoever had received the Spirit of Jesus Christ was esteemed a member of the church; now the order was inverted, and no one, unless a member of the church, was counted to have received the Spirit of Jesus Christ."

CHAPTER II.

Having made these preliminary remarks on the word Church, I come, now, to the matter in hand; and I shall lay down two propositions, which, I think, settle the whole question as to communion. The first of these propositions will be the subject of this chapter, and I thus state it. *While baptism is a personal, individual act, by which we confess Christ, the Lord's Supper is a social ordinance, belonging to the visible churches, and to be observed by these churches as churches.* This is the first of my propositions, and the arguments by which it is established, I now submit as compendiously as possible.

And, first, my first argument I find in the history of the institution of this ordinance. Observe the difference here between baptism and the supper. Jesus goes alone "from Galilee unto Jordan," and is baptized. Each apostle is baptized as an individual act, just as the Eunuch was. We find nothing social in this ordinance. But when the supper is instituted, there is preparation for a company. Messengers are sent to provide a convenient upper room. Here the Passover (a social repast— a sacred feast, to which *not fewer than ten persons were ever admitted,* Jahn. Arch. 354) was eaten. After this Passover, the Saviour instituted the supper. He and his disciples were a church, and in that church this ordinance begins. No one can read this account without feeling that the supper is a social ordinance, an entertainment *convivial* in its origin and character.

My second argument is drawn from the very name given in the Bible to this institution. It is called a supper, (*Deipnon*,) which was, among the ancients, the most social and convivial of all their repasts. In Matt. xxiii. 6, Mark, vi. 21, Luke, xiv. 16, and in many other passages, the same word means a banquet, a feast. This argument is enforced by 1 Cor. x. where this institution is called "a Communion." "The cup of blessing which we bless, is it not the communion of the blood of Christ? The bread which we break, is it not the cummunion of the body of Christ? For we, being many, are one bread and one body, for we are all partakers of that one bread." The reasoning of the apostle is this: As in partaking of the Lord's Supper we are united with Christians, so, if we partake of the heathen sacrificial feasts, we are joined with idolaters.

A third argument: It is the uniform practice of the apostolic age. Read the account of the revival on the day of Pentecost. This case is very important as the first precedent under the Commission; and what is the order there? First, "As many as gladly receive the word are baptized." What next? They are united to the Church in Jerusalem. "The same day there was added unto them about three thousand souls." After this, they participate in the supper. "And they continued steadfast in the apostle's doctrine, and fellowship, and in *breaking of bread*, and in prayer." (Acts, ii.)

We find the same practice mentioned in Acts, xx. 7.—"And upon the first day of the week, when the disciples *came together to break bread*, Paul preached unto them."

Baptism was administered on any day, and as individual subjects presented themselves; but the Supper was on Sunday, and the disciples came together that they might partake of it.

In the directions given to the churches, there is a fourth and conclusive argument as to the social character of the Eucharist. The fullest instructions which the New Testament furnishes on this topic are in the first Epistle to the Corinthians. In the eleventh chapter there are three passages bearing directly on the point before us. "When ye come together, therefore, into one place, this is not to eat the Lord's Supper. For in eating, every one taketh before other his own supper." "What! have ye not houses to eat and to drink in? or despise ye the church of God and shame them that have not?" "Wherefore, my brethren, when ye come together to eat, tarry one for another. And if any man hunger let him eat at home."

Now, here it is plain that the Supper was an institution in the church and for the church. When it was to be taken, *"they come together,"—come together for this very purpose.*

The members of the church were to wait for each other; that is, until all were assembled. To depart from this sacred courtesy, was a breach of respect, which the apostle condemns as "a contempt for the church." This church repast is contrasted with eating at home. Those private meals, individuals could take when moved by hunger; but in the Supper the members must wait for each other, and participate together.

I will only add, that the proposition I have submitted in this chapter, has ever been regarded as a theological axiom by all divines who have adopted the Bible as their body of divinity. I know there are ministers of the Gospel who have utterly degraded this ordinance, as well as baptism; who regard it as a means of conversion, thus placing it out of the church, and very much on the same footing with Anxious Seats. Others go even farther. They not only harangue against close communion, but practise a communion entirely promiscuous; inviting any body and every body. Pædobaptists, however, who make God's word their system, are shocked at this licentiousness.

Dr. Griffin (letter on Close Communion) says: "I agree with the advocates of close communion,"—"that we ought not to commune with those who are not baptized, and of course are not church members, even if we regard them as Christians. Should a pious Quaker so far depart from his principles as to wish to commune with me at the Lord's table, while yet he refused to be baptized, I could not receive him; because there is such a relationship established between the two ordinances, that I have no right to separate them; in other words, I have no right to send the sacred elements out of the church."

Dr. Dwight (Theol. v. iv. p. 365.)—"It is an indispensable qualification for the ordinance, that the candidate for communion be a member of the visible Church of Christ, in full standing."

CHAPTER III.

I HUMBLY conceive that I have established my first proposition, and proved that the supper is a social church ordinance; a spiritual repast, to be spread, not in the world, nor for the world, but in the visible churches, and for the members of those churches. Consequently no one can partake of the supper who is not a member in a visible church. I now advance my second proposition. It is this: *Baptism is a pre-requisite to admission into a visible church properly organized;* an assertion which would really seem scarcely to admit of argument.

A good deal of discussion has been wasted as to the baptism of those who first partook of the supper, viz: Christ and his apostles. Can any one doubt their baptism? First, we know that Jesus was baptized. The baptism of each of the apostles is not mentioned, nor would we expect that it should be; it is enough that all who followed John or Christ were baptized. In the next place, John's baptism was expressly "to make ready a people prepared for the Lord," and we know that Andrew was John's disciple (John i. 40;) is it supposable that the other eleven, chosen by Christ from among the Jews who flocked to John's baptism, were unbaptized? Thirdly, in selecting an apostle in the place of Judas, it is strongly intimated that the twelve had all been baptized by John. "Wherefore of these men which have companied with us all the time the Lord Jesus went in and out among us, beginning from the baptism of John, must one be taken." (Acts, i. 21, 22.) Fourthly, not only John's disciples, but those of Jesus, were all baptized, and they were employed by Christ to baptize others. "Jesus made and baptized more disciples than John, though Jesus himself baptized not, but his disciples." Is it possible those disciples were themselves unbaptized? In the fifth place, ponder those remarkable words of the Saviour, " Thus it becometh us to fulfill all righteousness." This he said of his own baptism; did he choose disciples who had not thus fulfilled all righteousness? In short, the apostles were never afterwards baptized; yet they were the persons sent under the Commission, to teach the world the duty of obeying this ordinance, and to baptize all nations. What would be thought of a minister who should go about preaching the Commission, and baptizing, and yet himself remain unbaptized?

Nor is there any force in the objection, that John's baptism was not Christian baptism. If, by Christian baptism, he meant baptism under the Commission, then the assertion is self-evident. But John's baptism was the baptism then instituted by God. It had reference prospectively to Christ, as baptism now points to him retrospectively; nor were those whom John had immersed afterwards immersed. I am not unmindful of the case at Ephesus (Acts, xix.) I believe there was a re-baptism there; but it was plainly on the ground that the rite had been administered in a manner grossly irregular, and without any proper instruction. They "had not even heard that there was any Holy Ghost." Were a person to apply now for membership, who had been immersed when so utterly unfit, I should regard his baptism very much as I do that of an infant. John's baptism was baptism. It was the baptism appointed by God. It was instituted before the supper, and those who first partook of the supper had been baptized. There is no sort of resemblance between them and those, in our day, who have not been baptized at all, but only sprinkled or poured upon.

In fact, however, the controversy as to John's baptism is of no sort of importance. We are, now, to be governed by the Commission, and the exposition of that document furnished by the example of the apostles. And, guided by these lights, can we, for a moment, doubt whether baptism is a pre-requisite to church membership; or whether it is to precede the supper? On this point the arguments are so numerous that my only embarrassment is in making a selection.

First, the Commission is peremptory, and this alone settles forever the question in hand. "Go teach all nations, baptizing them," and *then* "teaching them to observe all things whatsoever I have commanded you." Here there is required, first, *teaching*, (or as Mark has it, "*preaching the gospel*,") then, baptism; lastly, the persons thus converted and baptized are to be in a church, which is a school, where they are to be taught to observe all things commanded, of which things the supper is one.

A second argument is, the uniform practice under the Commission. On the day of Pentecost are the people told to repent and come to the Lord's table? Or, (as is now done, in violation of Christ's appointment) are they exhorted to come to the Lord's table, that they may repent and be converted? No. The apostle says, "**Repent** and be baptized." "Then as many as gladly received his word"—did what? received the supper? No. They "were baptized;" then they were added to the church, and participated in "breaking of bread."

The next illustration is found in Samaria. "When they believed Philip preaching the things concerning the kingdom of God, and the name of Jesus Christ, they" —what? received the supper? No. "They were baptized, both men and women."

When Saul asked, "Lord, what wilt thou have me to do?" he was directed to go into the city, and there his duty should be explained to him. He complies; and what is he told to do? To join the church? to receive the supper? No. He is commanded to be baptized. "And now why tarriest thou? Arise and be baptized, and wash away thy sins, calling on the name of the Lord."

Examine, thus, the cases of the Eunuch, the Jailor, Cornelius, and others, and you will find that baptism was always the first act after conversion.

The signification of the two ordinances furnishes a third argument as to their relative position. The church is supposed to be composed of those who profess to be born again; and the supper is *frequently* received, for it is emblematical of the constant nourishment which the spiritual life requires. But baptism is received only once. It is an emblem of the new birth. How preposterous, (I use the word in its strict sense—it is from *prepono* and intimates the putting something before, which ought to follow; as we say, putting the cart before the horse,) how preposterous to place the new life and its nourishment before the birth in which that new life began.

And this suggests a fourth argument. I mean the references constantly made to baptism, in which it is taken for granted that the members of churches have been baptized. These members have, of course, put on Christ; but the apostle says, "As many of you as have been baptized into Christ have put on Christ." When urging these members to holiness, a motive is fetched from their baptism: "Know ye not that so many of us as were baptized into Jesus Christ were baptized into his death? Therefore we are buried with him by baptism into death, that like as Christ was raised up from the dead by the glory of the Father, even so we also should walk in newness of life." When rebuking these members for divisions, an appeal is made to their baptism. "Were ye baptized in the name of Paul?" that is, in your baptism did you avow allegiance to man or to Christ? In short, observe "the proportion of faith," the order of those unities which bind the members of a Christian church to each other. "One Lord, one Faith, one Baptism, one God and Father of all, who is above all, and through all, and in you all."

But I am insisting too long upon this topic. If Christian churches, in all ages, have agreed touching any matter, it has been with reference to the proposition advanced in this chapter. They are unanimous in holding that baptism is a pre-requisite to church membership.

Ministers there are—I say it with grief—who admit into their churches people professing to be converted, or even wishing to be converted, and who never allude to baptism. I have baptized several persons who had been, for years, in churches, without either sprinkling, or pouring, or baptism. Nor is this a matter of surprise. What wonder if this solemn ordinance be treated with contempt by those who have degraded it into an unmeaning ceremony at the dedication of an infant.

But whatever some ministers may do, the voice of all churches is unequivocal upon this subject. Where is the church which would teach that in all cases members may be received without ever having been baptized? Every church would condemn this heresy, for it would be an abrogation of Christ's command. If, however, this ought not to be done in every case, it ought not to be done in any. By the standards of all churches, baptism is required before any candidate is admitted to membership; and this is the reason why baptism has always been regarded as a pre-requisite to the supper. The subjoined quotations are selected out of many.

"Before the grand Romish apostacy," says Mr. Booth, "in the very depths of that apostacy, and since the Reformation, both at home and abroad, the general practice has been to receive none but baptized persons to communion at the Lord's table." *

* Vindic. Part First.

Justin Martyr (A. D. 150,) Apol. ii. p. 162.—"This food is called by us the eucharist, of which it is not lawful for any to partake but such as believe the things that are taught by us to be true, and have been baptized."

Jerome (A. D. 400,) in cap. vi. ep. 2, ad Corinth.—"Catechumens cannot communicate at the Lord's table, being unbaptized."

Augustine (A. D. 400,) Epist. ad Boniface, ep. 106.—"Of which certainly they cannot partake unless they are baptized."

Bede (A. D. 700,) Hist. Eccles. Lib. ii. cap. 5, p. 63.—"Three young men, princes of the Eastern Saxons, seeing a bishop administer the sacred Supper, desired to partake of it as their royal father had done. To whom the bishop replied: If you will be baptized in the salutary fountain, as your father was, you may also partake of the Lord's Supper as he did; but if you despise the former, ye cannot, in any wise, receive the latter."

Theophylact (A. D. 1100,) cap. 4, Matt. p. 83.—"No unbaptized person partakes of the Lord's Supper."

Bonaventure (A. D. 1200,) Apud Forb. Instruct. Histor. Theol. lib. x. cap. 4.—"Faith, indeed, is necessary to all the sacraments, but especially to the reception of baptism, because baptism is the first among the sacraments, and the door to the sacraments."

Spanheim (A. D. 1600,) Hist. Christ. Col. 623.—"None but baptized persons are admitted to the Lord's table."

Lord Chancellor King (A. D. 1700,) Prim. Church, p. 196.—"Baptism was always precedent to the Lord's

Supper; and none (ever) were admitted to receive the eucharist till they were baptized. This is so obvious to every man that it needs no proof."

Dr. Wall, Inf. Bap. Part. ii. ch. ix.—"No church ever gave the communion to any persons before they were baptized. Among all the absurdities that ever were held, none ever maintained that any persons should partake of the communion before they were baptized."

Doddridge, Lectures, p. 510.—"It is certain that Christians in general have always been spoken of, by the most ancient Fathers, as baptized persons. And it is also certain that, as far as our knowledge of primitive antiquity extends, no unbaptized person received the Lord's Supper."

CHAPTER IV.

If my reader has followed me, I think he is now prepared to concede several things. I think he will grant that visible ordinances are for the visible churches; that the Supper is an institution for these visible churches, and to be received in them; and that baptism is prerequisite to admission into these visible churches. I do not see how either of these positions can be disputed. But, if these positions be granted, it follows inevitably that baptism is a pre-requisite to the Supper; and that we cannot admit to the Supper those whom we regard as unbaptized, however much we may love them, however deeply we lament the necessity laid upon us. To do this, would be to declare such persons qualified for membership in our churches; which would be to admit members without baptism; which would be to abolish baptism altogether.

May I be permitted here, without offence, in kindness and affection, to submit to the candor of our brethren another remark. Open communion, as it is called, requires us to admit to the Lord's table in our churches, the members of other churches. But, now, are not members admitted into some of these churches who are destitute of other qualifications for the Supper besides baptism?

Our brethren tell us, that all the infants baptized in their churches are church members; and are they displeased if we deny this. If, then, we are to receive to the Supper all their members, we must receive these infants as soon as they choose to come. No matter what their character when they grow up, the Pædobaptist churches do not excommunicate them; they are still members, and we must admit them. We must admit them, though the very churches in which they are pronounced to be members, would not!

But I shall be told that these are not the members referred to; it is the members in full standing in other churches, whom we ought to invite to the Lord's Supper. To which I answer, in all affection, thus:

First, in some of these churches all that is required,

after the baptism of the child, is confirmation by the prelate—another unscriptural rite, and administered, as we believe, by an unscriptural officer. After this confirmation the person is in full communion. Now, we dare not, as we love their souls, encourage people to receive the Lord's Supper who do not even profess to be converted. We dare not encourage disorder such as exists in these churches. Christ expressly requires teaching; then baptism; then membership. In these churches, the first teaching is expunged from the Commission; it is first, baptism; then teaching; then confirmation.

In other churches, persons are received and invited to the Supper, in order that they may be converted. Christ requires conversion, then baptism, then church-membership. In these churches, it is, first, baptism; then membership, and then conversion. How can we sanction this inversion and perversion of the order prescribed by Jesus?

I make these remarks reluctantly and with pain. I know, I rejoice to know, that in Pædobaptist Churches there are some of the noblest lights and ornaments of Christianity. With these we esteem it a privilege to enjoy the closest spiritual communion, and we only lament that they continue unbaptized. But while persons are admitted into some of these churches, as they are, without any profession of conversion, we cannot recognise church-membership in these bodies as conferring any sort of title to the Supper. Without conversion, people are proper subjects neither for the supper, nor for baptism. But I shorten this chapter, as the topics here discussed are ungenial to my heart, and may seem invidious to many for whom I cherish the sincerest esteem.

CHAPTER V.

I COME, in this chapter, to matters more pleasing, and proceed to consider briefly the objections usually urged against restricted communion.

Objection First. "Close communion betrays a want of fellowship with Christians of other denominations." But have I not already repelled this odious charge? Recall what I said of spiritual fellowship, the highest, noblest fellowship; a communion which transcends all mere communion in sensible emblems, as far as spirit transcends matter. In this glorious brotherhood we delight to feel ourselves one with all who truly love the Lord Jesus.

Let it not be said, then, that we want affection for our brethren. To be separated from them at the Lord's table is more painful to us, than to them; but our love for them, as well as our loyalty to Jesus, demands of us this self-denial.

What, in effect, is the remonstrance we continually address to our brethren? It is, that they are unbaptized. The more we admire their characters, so much more do we lament that they throw their influence on the side of error, and continue in disobedience. Now, in not inviting them to the Supper, our conduct only repeats this remonstrance; repeats it silently and kindly, but emphatically. To invite them would really be a want of love, for it would be an admission that they are baptized; and thus, in the strongest manner, we would contradict our declarations, and confirm them in error.

Objection Second. "God has received them, yet you will not." What does this mean? God is a Sovereign, and receives whom he will; but we are not; we are compelled to obey his regulations, and these forbid the unbaptized to partake of the Supper. "God receives them, and you hope to have communion with them in heaven." Be it so. I acquiesce. But what communion do you refer to? Is it in visible ordinances? Certainly not. It is spiritual communion, and this, as I have said, we enjoy with our brethren now.

To enforce this objection, the language of Peter (Acts, xv. 8) is sometimes cited: "And God, which knoweth the hearts, bare them witness, giving them the Holy Ghost, even as he did unto us. And put no difference between us and them, purifying their heart by faith. Now, therefore, why tempt ye God to put a yoke upon the neck of the disciples, which neither our fathers nor we were able to bear? But we believe that through the grace of the Lord Jesus Christ we shall be saved, even as they."

Such was Peter's address. But what has it to do with the question I am discussing? The sacred historian is recording a case in which certain Pharisees who

THE TERMS OF COMMUNION. 241

had been converted, wished to compel the Gentile converts to be circumcised. Peter says, No, God makes no difference between Jew and Gentile under the gospel, and you have no authority to require of the Gentile a painful Jewish rite. The case proves incontestably that baptism did not come in the room of circumcision; since the Jewish Christians not only retained the latter rite, but wished to impose it on the Gentile Christians. But where is the analogy between our conduct and the antichristian exaction of these Pharisees?

In requiring baptism, we only obey what we and our brethren admit to be the command of Christ. Suppose a case. Suppose that in the days of the apostles any one had refused to be baptized, can we doubt what would have been his treatment? Who believes that such a candidate would have been admitted into any of the churches? Nor would it have availed him to protest that he did not regard baptism as essential, or that he had been sprinkled and regarded that as baptism. Had such a case occurred and been recorded, I am persuaded that, instead of a welcome to the Lord's table, we should have heard, from apostolic lips, a rebuke far more stern than any which we have the heart or the right to administer.*

* I am sorry to find such a man as Baptist Noel advocating open communion, because in the days of the apostles there could have been no doubt as to baptism. This concedes that the Scriptures are obscure on that subject; an assertion which would be a libel on the Bible, an insult to God, and which meets abundant refutation in Mr. Noel's own work. We have in the New Testament all that God saw it was necessary to say; all that the apostles would say, if they were now on earth.

242 THE TERMS OF COMMUNION.

Objection Third. "Pædobaptists are sincere, and if sincere, their error, supposing there is error, ought to be tolerated." "Him that is weak in the faith receive ye." This is the third objection, and I wish I could see any force in it.

This plea strips the churches of all right to judge as to the qualification of those admitted to the Supper. If a man only be sincere, the church is to regard sincerity in error as a substitute for obedience to the truth. "Him that is weak in faith," we gladly receive. However feeble the Christian be, if his faith lead him to obey Christ and be baptized, we will welcome him into our churches, and pray that his soul may there be nourished and confirmed. But disobedience and weak faith are very different things; and a church which should sanction disobedience, because sincere, would subvert the whole gospel.

Far be it from me to impeach the sincerity of any body; but God has conferred upon no man, nor body of men, a tolerating power. To exercise such a power, is arrogantly to usurp God's prerogative. If God requires baptism before the Supper, who will dare to dispense with it?

The very word "tolerate" supposes error. But, now, if our brethren are in error, what is the duty of the churches towards them? As far ss I am concerned, my duty is clear. I am to love my brother—to remember that I am prone to err—above all, not to persecute him, as if I were his master, for "to his own master he standeth or falleth." My duty, my heart, bids me cherish towards my brother that charity which "hopeth all things, believeth all things," and which, with affectionate solicitude, will seek to turn my brother from the error of his way.

But the duty of the churches is equally plain. The order established by Christ requires baptism before the Supper. If a church violate this order, it is not only faithless to Christ, but to an immortal soul; a soul which, by this church act, is confirmed in disobedience.

Objection Fourth. "It is the Lord's table." I answer, yes; and this is the very reason why we dare not admit those who have not the pre-requisite which the Lord requires. Were it our table we would give vent to our feelings, and joyfully invite our brethren. But it is the Lord's table. The Lord, himself, has prescribed the regulations as to his own table; and a minister has no right to act as master of ceremonies, and extend invitations to whom he will. The Lord has fenced around his table; who will venture to break down the enclosure? He orders that the baptized only shall communicate; who will dare to abrogate this order?

Objection Fifth. "The Baptists are inconsistent, for they unite with their Pædobaptist brethren in prayer meetings, and even invite them into their pulpits, and yet exclude them from the Lord's Supper." What, however, would our brethren wish to take by this objection?

Suppose I admit the inconsistency, what would follow? Not, surely, that we ought to receive unbaptized persons to the Supper, but that we ought not to unite with them in acts of religious worship at all. And would our brethren desire to force us to such a conclusion? Would they wish to sunder us altogether from those we love? If they could harbor such a thought, I tell them here at once they will be defeated. We will endure their upbraidings for inconsistency; but we will not be divorced from those who deserve and possess so much of our affection. We will pray with them; we will invite them into our pulpits, and gladly sit at their feet while they preach that Christ whom they love and we love; and if they will still reproach us as inconsistent, be it so. We can forgive their taunts, but we will deprecate and resist the issue to which those taunts would drive us, exclaiming, in tones of most earnest expostulation, "What mean ye, thus to break our hearts?"

More than this, however, we cannot do. It is written in the book of Kings, that when all else failed to seduce the young prophet from the word of God, he yielded to the influence of the old prophet. And if any thing could tempt us to depart from the Saviour's injunction, it would be our regard and esteem for our brethren of other communions. But we must not thus be seduced. We must deny ourselves. We can bear the charge of inconsistency; but to admit unbaptized persons to the Supper would not only be inconsistency, in us it would be deliberate sin.

Thus far I have been supposing some inconsistency;

but, in fact, the charge is wholly unfounded. Baptism is no pre-requisite to prayer or benevolence. I can kneel, I can co-operate, with any who love Jesus, and who seek to diffuse the knowledge of salvation. So, too, as to preaching. I look with pity, I had almost said, with contempt, at the Puseyism which invests an edifice built for worship with any superstitious sanctity; which erects an altar in a Christian chapel; and regards a pulpit as a sort of holiest of holies. All this, to my mind, is Romanism, and greatly degrades the simple glory of the gospel. To me, with my Bible before me, such an edifice is only a house erected for the accommodation of worshippers; and the pulpit is only a platform for the convenience of the preacher. If a man preach falsehood, I would shut him out of the pulpit, though he had been baptized in the Jordan, and though the Pope and the whole college of Cardinals had put their hands on his head. But if a man preach the truth as it is in Jesus, I would feel no sort of scruple about his occupying the pulpit, though he were unbaptized.

I would feel no sort of scruple about his occupying the pulpit, though he were unbaptized; but unbaptized, he could not be invited to the Lord's Table. This would be a very different thing from his standing in the pulpit to speak. In this the church would receive him to an ordinance placed by Christ within those precincts which none are permitted to enter until after baptism.

There is only one more Objection to our terms of communion. It is that we "unchurch other denominations." But, after what has been said, I need scarcely notice this accusation. If it be intended that we consider these churches as not in the order of the gospel, the charge is true. They do not keep the ordinances as they have been delivered by Christ. Nor, as we love them and love Christ, would we withhold the silent but kind admonition uttered by the very restriction which they condemn. But we have already said that any society, formed for religious worship, is a church; and the zeal, and devotion, and efficiency, of many Pædobaptist Churches, fill us with admiration and joy.

CHAPTER VI.

This chapter concludes our essay. In finishing, I wish to recall the verse which I placed, as a motto, at the head of this part of my subject, and to answer the question it proposes. "*But we desire to hear of thee what thou thinkest;* for as concerning this sect, we know that every where it is spoken against." I have considered the charge of illiberality so universally alleged against us. In replying, now, to the inquiry in this passage, and saying what I think, let me be pardoned for speaking in the first person. I shall, thus, express my own feelings in a manner the most concise, direct, and unreserved.

I do think, then, that to speak against the Baptists for

their practice in communion is not right. It is unkind; since this separation from our brethren is more painful to us than it can be to them. It is unjust; since the true, the only difference between our practice and theirs is in baptism—their churches not admitting to the Supper any whom they regard as unbaptized. It is ungenerous; since not only love to Christ, but to our brethren, imposes on us this severe duty. In short, these invectives are most mischievous; serving, not to promote truth and peace, but to turn away many from searching for truth, and to exasperate some of the worst passions of the human heart.

I think, if we look at facts, we will admit that this clamor about close communion is, after all, without a cause, and deserves no better name than *croaking*. Our brethren boast that they invite all; but, in truth, how often do they commune together? How often do our Methodist and Presbyterian brethren commune together? How often do the Lutherans and Episcopalians commune together? Nay, take those who bear the same name, and tell me, do the New School and the Old School Presbyterian churches, do the Methodist Episcopal and the Methodist Protestant churches, often commune? In point of fact, each of the churches has its communion seasons, and the members, at those times, commune. Why, then, such an outcry against us for not admitting those to the Supper, who, if admitted, would seldom or never come?

A third reflection. While I deplore the existence of any barrier which walls us off from those we love, yet the fault is not ours. We neither erected, nor can we remove the barrier. In order to church fellowship, God requires certain unities. There must be "one Lord, one faith, one baptism." We rejoice that in the two first unities we harmonize with our brethren. Let them return to the baptism of the Bible, and all separation will cease. Until then they, and not we, are responsible for the divisions which exist. When Ahab said to Elijah, "Art thou he that troubleth Israel? the prophet well replied, I have not troubled Israel, but thou and thy father's house, in that thou hast forsaken the commandments of the Lord."

I think if the mind of Christ be in us, we will still be joined in heart, though as to ordinances we may not agree. Whereas, if we have not the spirit of Christ, there would be no union, even should we touch each other at the Lord's table.

Lastly, in such a state as the present, I think, and my readers will think with me, that Christians ought to love one another, notwithstanding some discrepancies in their views. This life is not an economy of perfect light. It is holiness, not knowledge, which we are here to perfect. "Now we know in part;" such is the declaration of God; and in this truth there is an emphasis that ought for ever to silence those anathemas which, for so many ages, Christians have been fulminating against each other.

That we agree in so much, for this let us thank God. That we disagree as to baptism is greatly to be lamented. It shews that there is error somewhere; nor should we esteem any error a light thing, nor regard him as otherwise than our enemy, who would lull us to sleep in error. These very difficulties between professed Christians admonish us to cease from man, and to make the Bible our guide. Let us take heed to this warning. The ancient legend says, that when the heathen deity Jupiter was born, his priests filled the air with their shouts, that the cries of the god might be drowned. This fable is too just a satire on the controversies and clamors which now create such a din in the theological world. Every sect tells you, indeed, to go to Christ; but each shouts, "Christ is here." All proclaim their own creeds and articles so loudly and vehemently, that the voice of the Great Teacher can scarcely be heard.

Let us not listen to these artificers of religion, these heralds and partisans of human creeds and standards. Let us repair to the Bible. Let us go to Jesus himself, and sit down at his feet, and learn of him with meek, and willing, and submissive hearts. Until we thus seek, we cannot be surprised that differences exist; nor can we have any good evidence that we are Christians. In other days the whole difficulty was *to obey* the truth. At present, amidst the jarring conflicts of parties, and passions, and prejudices, it often craves a magnanimous soul even *to know what the truth is*. Oh that, with a Berean spirit, all Christians were searching the Scriptures. Come that day, and at once all discord would vanish, and the earth be peopled and blessed with peace, and love, and joy.

We must not, however, expect too much in such a world. The present economy is one of darkness and nescience. Our knowlege here is but another sort of ignorance. The known only conducts us to the unknown. The very light only discovers fathomless abysses. "Now we know in part." Let this truth correct all arrogance as to our own views; let it teach us to suspect ourselves, and to be lenient to others. Above all, let us learn to lift our eyes to heaven, and to long for another economy; an economy of light and knowledge. Here what blindness! what imperfection! what selfishness! what dissensions among those who ought to love one another even as Christ also loved them!

But thus it shall not always be. Soon we shall soar far away from these sources of sorrow and humiliation. Soon "we shall know, even also as we are known." "When I was a child, I spake as a child, I understood as a child, I thought as a child." Such is the metaphor by which the apostle describes the attainments of the most advanced Christians, in the present state. But another state will succeed. "When I became a man, I put away childish things." In heaven, among "the saints of light," all these puerilities, these imbecilities of childhood, shall be superseded; all these imperfections which now tarnish the Christian's character, and defeat his warmest aspirations, shall be cast off. There, truth will reign supreme. There, no tear shall ever dim the eye, no darkness ever obscure the mind, no passion ever sully the immortal soul. There, all who love and obey Jesus shall, in all things, be one; shall all be called by one name; all be clothed in one glittering uniform; all sit down to the marriage supper of the

Lamb, that high festival of purity and love; and all sweep the full diapason of glory, singing, with one heart and one voice, that new song which once begun shall never end, "Unto Him that hath loved us, and washed us from our sins in his own blood, and hath made us kings and priests unto God and his Father, to Him be glory and dominion for ever and ever. Amen."

"Now the God of peace, that brought again from the dead our Lord Jesus, that great Shepherd of the sheep, through the blood of the everlasting covenant, make us perfect in every good work to do his will, working in us that which is well-pleasing in his sight, through Jesus Christ, to whom be glory for ever and ever. Amen."

THE END.

A
Biographical Sketch
of
Richard Fuller
(1804-1876)

By
John Franklin Jones

A Biographical Sketch of Richard Fuller (1804-1876)

Richard Fuller—lawyer, pastor, denominational leader, author—was born April 22, 1804 in Beaufort, South Carolina (Armitage), the ninth of ten children born to Thomas and Elizabeth Middleton Fuller. His parents became Baptists about the time of his birth, but he was brought up more Episcopalian than anything else.

Fuller married Charlotte Bull in 1831. He was converted shortly thereafter (*ESB*) in 1831 at Beaufort. Concerning his conversion, he said, "My soul ran over with love and joy and praise; for days I could neither eat nor sleep." He was baptized by Rev. H. O. Wyer, of Savannah, and united with the Baptist church at his native place (Armitage).

He studied at Harvard, but broken health required his leaving in his junior year. Returning after five years, he graduated at the head of his class in 1824 (Armitage), being awarded a diploma for his past good record (*ESB*).

Fuller studied law and rose to eminence in the profession. He left his lucrative law business, was ordained in 1832 (Armitage), and became pastor at Beaufort. He remained there for fifteen years (*ESB*) and grew the feeble church to 200 white and 2400 colored. He also conducted an itinerant ministry, brought great numbers to Christ, and traveled to Europe for his health in 1836 (Armitage).

He felt that Scripture sanctioned the practice of slavery and explained his belief in an article for the *Christian Reflector*, Philadelphia. His fellow Baptist, Francis Wayland, countered, and a long argument ensued. Fuller's views were published in *Domestic Slavery Considered as a Scriptural Institution* (1845) (*ESB*).

In 1847, Fuller became pastor of Seventh Baptist Church, Baltimore and continued therein throughout the Civil War until 1871 (*ESB*). The church numbered eighty-seven members at the time and grew to 1200 during his tenure (Armitage). He held together a congregation whose congregants fought for both North and South (*ESB*).

He served as president of the Maryland Baptist Union Association (1850) and thrice preached its annual sermon (1847, 1855, 1859). Fuller preached the first annual sermon ever preached at the Southern Baptist Convention (1846) and was president of the Southern Baptist Convention twice (1859, 1861). At the 1869 Convention, he spoke in favor of forming Southern Baptist Theological Seminary. In a 1872 address on domestic missions, he advocated work among Negroes (*ESB*).

Fuller led the Provisional Board in Baltimore during the Civil War. That board continued the denomination's foreign mission work during the war and served the denomination when the Foreign Mission Board in Richmond when communication with missionaries located in China and Africa was cut off and when funds from the South were unavailable (*ESB*).

He and several members from the Seventh Church formed the Eutaw Place Baptist Church in 1871. He served as its pastor until his death (*ESB*).

Fuller authored *Baptism and the Terms of Communion: An Argument* (1854). He penned *Sermons* (1860). He wrote *A City or House Divided Against Itself. A Discourse*

A Biographical Sketch of Richard Fuller

Delivered...on the First Day of June, 1865, Being the Day of National Fasting and Humiliation (1865). Twenty-nine years of his sermons are contained in *Sermons Delivered...During His Ministry with the Seventh and Eutaw Churches, Baltimore, 1847-76* (1877). With J. B. Jeter, he published an edition of *The Psalmist* (1843), adding a supplement to make it more acceptable to Baptist churches in the South (*ESB*).

Fuller was appreciated nationwide as a preacher and he was strongly committed to divine inspiration. He was a painstaking student, an able pastor, and widely recognized as an extemporaneous preacher and master orator (Armitage). He died in Baltimore, Maryland October 20, 1876 (*ESB*).

BIBLIOGRAPHY

Armitage, Thomas. *A History of the Baptists; Traced by their Vital Principles and Practices, from the Time of Our Lord and Saviour Jesus Christ to the Year 1886*. With an introduction by J. L. M. Curry. New York: Bryan, Taylor, & Co. 1887, 760-62.

Encyclopedia of Southern Baptists. S.v. "Fuller, Richard," by C. Clyde Atkins.

BY JOHN FRANKLIN JONES
CORDOVA, TENNESSEE
JUNE 2004

THE BAPTIST STANDARD BEARER, INC.

a non-profit, tax-exempt corporation
committed to the Publication & Preservation
of the Baptist Heritage.

CURRENT TITLES AVAILABLE IN
THE BAPTIST *DISTINCTIVES* SERIES

KIFFIN, WILLIAM — A Sober Discourse of Right to Church-Communion. Wherein is proved by Scripture, the Example of the Primitive Times, and the Practice of All that have Professed the Christian Religion: That no Unbaptized person may be Regularly admitted to the Lord's Supper. (London: George Larkin, 1681).

KINGHORN, JOSEPH — Baptism, A Term of Communion. (Norwich: Bacon, Kinnebrook, and Co., 1816)

KINGHORN, JOSEPH — A Defense of "Baptism, A Term of Communion". In Answer To Robert Hall's Reply. (Norwich: Wilkin and Youngman, 1820).

GILL, JOHN — Gospel Baptism. A Collection of Sermons, Tracts, etc., on Scriptural Authority, the Nature of the New Testament Church and the Ordinance of Baptism by John Gill. (Paris, AR: The Baptist Standard Bearer, Inc., 2006).

CARSON, ALEXANDER	Ecclesiastical Polity of the New Testament. (Dublin: William Carson, 1856).
BOOTH, ABRAHAM	A Defense of the Baptists. A Declaration and Vindication of Three Historically Distinctive Baptist Principles. Compiled and Set Forth in the Republication of Three Books. Revised edition. (Paris, AR: The Baptist Standard Bearer, Inc., 2006).
BOOTH, ABRAHAM	Paedobaptism Examined on the Principles, Concessions, and Reasonings of the Most Learned Paedobaptists. With Replies to the Arguments and Objections of Dr. Williams and Mr. Peter Edwards. 3 volumes. (London: Ebenezer Palmer, 1829).
CARROLL, B. H.	*Ecclesia* - The Church. With an Appendix. (Louisville: Baptist Book Concern, 1903).
CHRISTIAN, JOHN T.	Immersion, The Act of Christian Baptism. (Louisville: Baptist Book Concern, 1891).
FROST, J. M.	Pedobaptism: Is It From Heaven Or Of Men? (Philadelphia: American Baptist Publication Society, 1875).
FULLER, RICHARD	Baptism, and the Terms of Communion; An Argument. (Charleston, SC: Southern Baptist Publication Society, 1854).
GRAVES, J. R.	Tri-Lemma: or, Death By Three Horns. The Presbyterian General Assembly Not Able To Decide This Question: "Is Baptism In The Romish Church Valid?" 1st Edition.

	(Nashville: Southwestern Publishing House, 1861).
MELL, P.H.	Baptism In Its Mode and Subjects. (Charleston, SC: Southern Baptist Publications Society, 1853).
JETER, JEREMIAH B.	Baptist Principles Reset. Consisting of Articles on Distinctive Baptist Principles by Various Authors. With an Appendix. (Richmond: The Religious Herald Co., 1902).
PENDLETON, J.M.	Distinctive Principles of Baptists. (Philadelphia: American Baptist Publication Society, 1882).
THOMAS, JESSE B.	The Church and the Kingdom. A New Testament Study. (Louisville: Baptist Book Concern, 1914).
WALLER, JOHN L.	Open Communion Shown to be Unscriptural & Deleterious. With an introductory essay by Dr. D. R. Campbell and an Appendix. (Louisville: Baptist Book Concern, 1859).

For a complete list of current authors/titles, visit our internet site at:
www.standardbearer.org
or write us at:

he Baptist Standard Bearer, Inc.

NUMBER ONE IRON OAKS DRIVE • PARIS, ARKANSAS 72855
TEL # 479-963-3831   *FAX # 479-963-8083*
EMAIL: Baptist@centurytel.net   http://www.standardbearer.org

Thou hast given a standard to them that fear thee; that it may be displayed because of the truth. — Psalm 60:4

www.ingramcontent.com/pod-product-compliance
Lightning Source LLC
Chambersburg PA
CBHW021806220426
43662CB00006B/195